TABLE OF CONTENTS

ACRONYMS

A2AD	Anti-Access / Area Denial
ASHA	American Schools and Hospitals Abroad
CJCS	Chairman of the Joint Chiefs of Staff
COCOM	Combatant Command
DOD	Department of Defense
FMS	Foreign Military Sales
IR	International Relations
JP	Joint Publication
MOI	Ministry of Interior
NATO	North Atlantic Treaty Organization
NPT	Non-Proliferation Treaty
NWFZ	Nuclear-Weapons-Free Zone
QME	Qualitative Military Edge
R2P	Responsibility to Protect
ROK	Republic of Korea
SECDEF	Secretary of Defense
UK	United Kingdom
UN	United Nations
UNSC	United Nations Security Council
UNSCR	United Nations Security Council Resolution
USAF	United States Air Force
USG	United States Government
WMD	Weapon(s) of Mass Destruction

INTRODUCTION

Right, as the world goes, is only in question between equals in power, while the strong do what they can and the weak suffer what they must.

—Thucydides, 416 BC

Centuries ago and for several to follow, legitimacy emanated from the power of coercive military strength, whereby might made right and the victor set the standards of legitimacy.[1] Ancient Greek historian Thucydides described this dynamic in his account of the Peloponnesian War, suggesting no single Greek *polis* (city-state) monopolized or enjoyed military might for long.[2] Rather, lasting military might typically materialized in the form and context of alliances, formal or otherwise.[3] Regardless of the reasons behind their formation or the intent they were to serve, alliances gradually became the normalized mechanism to bolster national strength, secure access and resources, and confer collective consent-based legitimacy. In short, there evolved an inextricable link between alliances and legitimacy with respect to military action, a relationship that Thucydides chronicled long ago and one that is still quite prevalent today.

For the United States, alliances continue to serve a vital role in fulfilling its national security interests, a reality the President of the United States notably reinforced in his 2012 Defense Strategic Guidance.[4] In particular, they provide additional means by which the U.S. military pursues its operational objectives in support of national security requirements and

---

[1] Rudolph C. Barnes, Jr., *Military Legitimacy: Might and Right in the New Millennium* (London: Frank Cass, 1996), 5.

[2] Thucydides, *The Landmark Thucydides: A Comprehensive Guide to the Peloponnesian War* (New York: Free Press, 1998), xviii.

[3] The author intends to clarify the difference between formal and informal alliances (the latter of which are more often coined strategic partnerships) during the course of this monograph, but will commonly refer to all such international relationships as 'alliances'.

[4] U.S. Department of Defense, *2012 U.S. Department of Defense Strategic Guidance* (Washington, DC: U.S. Department of Defense, 2012), 3.

strategic interests. Alliances provide additional human and material resources to augment the U.S. military's combat power. They also enable access into regions otherwise impermissible without violating the sovereignty of foreign nations or severely straining—if not exceeding—its operational reach.[5] More importantly though, especially given the topic of this monograph, alliances often serve to legitimate U.S. military actions, particularly when such actions appear to defy existing international laws. The collective nature of alliances, particularly when exercised in the form of international military coalitions, lends considerable credibility to the legitimacy narrative used to justify coercive action in contested situations.[6] Moreover, alliances offer an additional or alternate source of authority to confer legitimacy upon prudent military action otherwise constrained by the straitjacket of legalism.[7]

Meanwhile, the U.S. military considers legitimacy a critical ingredient—if not a decisive factor—to succeed in its operations, identifying it within core doctrine as one of the twelve principles of joint operations.[8] Whether it form the backdrop of stability operations in a counterinsurgency campaign or justify the use of force to topple an oppressive regime and prevent the proliferation of weapons of mass destruction (WMD), legitimacy is arguably a

---

[5]This statement assumes deliberate violations of national sovereignty by the U.S. military—while necessary at times to pursue distinct national security objectives—is neither desired nor lightly considered as a matter of habitual occurrence. On the contrary, the sovereignty of nations is largely respected and permission to trespass into sovereign territory is always pursued unless doing so would compromise the need for surprise and speed in achieving a specific national security objective.

[6]Richard Falk, Mark Juergensmeyer, and Vesselin Popovski, eds., *Legality and Legitimacy in Global Affairs* (New York: Oxford University Press, 2012), 439.

[7]Ibid.

[8]U.S. Department of Defense, Joint Chiefs of Staff, *JP 3-0, Joint Operations* (Washington, DC: Government Printing Office, August 2011), A-4. In 2008, three additional principles—restraint, perseverance, and legitimacy—joined the original nine principles of war to comprise the twelve principles of joint operations currently referenced in JP 3-0.

military force multiplier and fundamental requirement in the modern operational environment.[9] It not only enhances the perceived credibility of U.S. military forces operating in contested areas, but also facilitates voluntary compliance by the host nation, thereby reducing the coercive "enforcement and surveillance" costs typically associated with securing and policing a contested operational environment.[10] The principles and sources of authority upon which the legitimacy narrative takes shape range from norms of morality and human rights to international law, codified and theoretically enforced by impartial organizations like the United Nations Security Council (UNSC).[11] Legitimacy also seems highly dependant on perceived notions of consistent state behavior in the international arena as well as transparent motivations behind national actions. In other words, legitimacy is stronger and more lasting when perceived actions match words, and when those actions and words do not betray ulterior motives. Quite simply, legitimacy is an indispensable component of U.S. military operations.

---

[9]The author suggests legitimacy was an important ingredient leveraged by the USG to justify its military operations in Afghanistan and Iraq between 2001 and 2012. Specifically, the author contends that legitimacy afforded credibility to U.S. military forces who interacted with the Afghan population and tried to secure their trust in order to conduct security and stability operations within its broader counterinsurgency strategy. As for military operations in Iraq, the author suggests legitimacy—derived from the moral argument and international imperative of curbing mass atrocities committed by a tyrannical regime as well as preventing the proliferation of WMD in a volatile region like the Middle East—provided the initial justification for its 2003 invasion and subsequent toppling of the Saddam Hussein regime.

[10]Ian Hurd, "Legitimacy and Authority in International Politics," *International Organization* 53, no. 2 (Spring 1999): 384.

[11]Falk, Juergensmeyer, and Popovski, eds., *Legality and Legitimacy in Global Affairs*, 48. In theory, the neutrality of the UN enables it to arbitrate disputes between or among nations. However, its neutrality is often called into question by critics who claim the hierarchical nature and disparate power of its constituents conflict with its ability to remain neutral. This situation is particularly evident in the UN Security Council where its permanent member countries (also known as the P5+1)—China, Russia, France, Germany, the United Kingdom, and the United States—each have veto power to overrule any organizational agenda. This criticism is a source of ongoing debate over the relevance and role of the UNSC, and will be discussed in more detail later in this monograph.

The Challenge for the U.S. Military

In many ways, the ability to uphold and reinforce legitimacy exists within the U.S. military's capacity, whether achieved by exhibiting tactical and operational restraint or by adhering to objectives agreed upon by the international community.[12] Conversely, the ability to pursue and secure alliances and, in turn, the legitimacy they beget falls primarily on the shoulders of America's foreign diplomats and senior governmental officials, and ultimately the President of the United States. This is not to say the military bears no responsibility or has no influence in America's alliance strategy. On the contrary, senior military leaders, specifically the Joint Chiefs of Staff and COCOM Commanders, contribute greatly toward shaping alliances. They do so by way of the advice they provide to the nation's top civilian leadership, namely the Secretary of Defense (SECDEF) and, more importantly, the President of the United States. It is to suggest, however, that alliances are rarely pursued and secured with only military interests in mind; rather, there are a myriad of other factors and national interests that drive alliances, which may not always complement specific military interests. This creates significant tension between the nation's policymakers and their subordinate policy 'shapers'. It also serves to highlight part of the challenge facing the U.S. military: it must function within the alliance structure and legitimacy milieu that America's foreign policy creates. Moreover, the U.S. military must work with an alliance framework that may or may not serve its operational needs, and with allies who may or may not support its legitimacy.

This dynamic points to a significant challenge for U.S. military commanders and planners alike, and the fundamental question this monograph intends to answer: how to navigate an operational environment characterized by contradictory alliances that potentially undermine U.S. military legitimacy. The answer is no more easily revealed than is the nature of the environment

---

[12]U.S. Department of Defense, Joint Chiefs of Staff, *JP 3-0, Joint Operations*, A-4.

4

in which the U.S. military will operate in the near future. What is certain, though, is that alliances and legitimacy will play an integral role in most, if not all, future U.S. military operations. Additionally, tension will remain between the two—alliances and legitimacy—as America's national security interests beget strategic partnerships that are often at odds with America's claims of legitimacy. The key to navigating such an operational environment is, first, to identify the potential conflicts or friction points between alliances and legitimacy. Once identified, military commanders and planners must negotiate an acceptable balance between the two factors. They must determine which is more important to the success of its operations: the added resources afforded by alliances or the benefit of a stronger and more resilient foundation of legitimacy upon which to conduct its operations. In turn, they must expect and accept that the prioritization of one will likely compromise the other. They must account for the ramifications of such decisions when planning and performing their operations; this monograph will highlight many of those ramifications. Furthermore, planners and commanders alike must influence the resulting narrative that describes and directs the optimum balance between these two aspects, ensuring each contribute materially to the achievement of both operational and strategic objectives. In the end, if alliances do more to hinder than help U.S. military operations, particularly with respect to legitimacy, then they should take steps to mitigate the delegitimizing damage they inflict. However, if possible, such steps should stop short of undermining the vital role that alliances play in securing America's national interests.

Once again, it is well within the capacity of the U.S. military to meet and overcome such a challenge, particularly if it develops a thorough understanding of both legitimacy and alliances, and accounts for each throughout the entire operations process. At a time when unilateral action is not only unfeasible but also unacceptable to the world community, it requires U.S. military commanders and planners to intentionally develop and implement an operational approach that properly balances the costs and benefits of its alliances with the risks and rewards to its legitimacy.[13] This may require counterintuitive—even countercultural—solutions in devising an

approach that suits this purpose.[14] Moreover, it may require suboptimal measures and operational

concessions in order to conserve U.S. military power and invest in long-term legitimacy.[15]

Indeed, incurring greater short-term costs via an approach that attenuates U.S. military reliance on

policy-directed alliances, particularly those that appear to contradict America's stated ideals, may

yield huge dividends in terms of long-term legitimacy, especially when legitimacy plays an

integral role in the ease or success of its military operations. This is, therefore, not simply a good

idea. Rather, it is a mandate for commanders and planners charged with walking this operational

tightrope: developing and implementing an approach that preserves legitimacy while remaining

nested with policy-driven alliance strategies.

Monograph Purpose and Approach

This monograph seeks to examine the quandary once articulated by Thucydides as it

applies today: navigating the complex operational environment while securing and maintaining

alliances—whether congruent with American ideals or not—and, if possible, simultaneously

securing and maintaining legitimacy. It does so by first defining and developing the concept of

legitimacy, explaining the sources of authority from which it derives, and the reasons behind its

elusiveness. It then proceeds to define alliances, differentiating them from partnerships in terms

---

[13]Elizabeth Sherwood-Randall, *Alliances and American National Security* (Carlisle Barracks: SSI, U.S. Army War College, 2006), 14.

[14]The author suggests the U.S. military typically chooses the most efficient path possible to gain and preserve access to regions of military interest and, in doing so, will either opportunistically build relationships with partner nations or willfully violate their sovereignty to serve that purpose. In effect, this is a cultural standard of practice for U.S. military operations. By 'counterculture', the author refers to solutions that do not adhere to this standard operating practice.

[15]G. John Ikenberry, *After Victory: Institutions, Strategic Restraint, and the Rebuilding of Order After Major Wars* (Princeton: Princeton University Press, 2001), 53.

of their formality and durability. It also examines the role of alliances, be it to bolster or erode legitimacy (i.e. cost-benefit relationship), and briefly reviews the motivations behind their formation, the factors that influence their dependability and longevity, and the causes of their ultimate dissolution. Finally, it addresses ways in which military commanders and planners may account for legitimacy as they develop and implement their operational approach, ensuring it remains interwoven throughout the operations process and fully synchronized with the strategic calculus of policy-driven alliances. It is this final point that bears the greatest relevance and interest to the reader of this monograph if, in fact, legitimacy is truly as integral to operational success for the U.S. military as its doctrine suggests.[16] Furthermore, recent history indicates the U.S. military must be ready to conduct operations abroad, often alongside allies and partners whose contributions are important if not decisive, with or without a firm foundation of legitimacy underlying such operations. Consequently, it is in the interest of the U.S. military—a force repeatedly called upon to navigate complex operational environments—to develop a better understanding of legitimacy and how to integrate it into the entire operations process. It must ensure its operational approach aptly leverages the benefits of alliances but shrewdly mitigates the risks those alliances sometimes pose to its legitimacy.

This monograph does not attempt to debate the existence or relevance of legitimacy, though it addresses both topics in the course of discussion as a means of identifying why legitimacy is so difficult to consistently secure and maintain. Additionally, this monograph will neither refute nor reinforce the long-standing notion that tactical actions have strategic effects with respect to U.S. military legitimacy. Consequently, the reader will find no discussion of such notorious delegitimizing events as the Abu Ghraib prisoner abuse case in Iraq or the religious and cultural transgressions that periodically surface in Afghanistan (e.g. allegations of torture and

---

[16]U.S. Department of Defense, Joint Chiefs of Staff, *JP 3-0, Joint Operations*, A-4.

extraordinary rendition, desecration of Muslim corpses or the Qur'an, etc.).[17] Furthermore, this monograph will not engage in a lengthy debate over the perceived hypocrisy of American foreign policy and, more specifically, the perception that the U.S. cherry-picks among international norms and laws to justify its selective use of military force.[18] Rather, it will briefly acknowledge this common criticism as an antagonist to U.S. military legitimacy. Finally, this monograph will not argue the merits of one alliance over another. America's alliances ostensibly serve some necessary function or interest, regardless of whether or not they facilitate U.S. military operations or reinforce its legitimacy. Consequently, commanders and planners must nest their operational approach within the framework of alliances and partnerships negotiated by the U.S. government as a whole. This does not, however, mean the military must hold its doctrinal mandate on legitimacy subordinate to its operational use of alliances, or lack thereof.

Ultimately, in terms of the discourse on legitimacy, there are those who question its utility—even its existence—on the one hand, and those who consider it paramount to the conduct of military operations on the other. The reality probably lies somewhere in between. While alliances often advance national interests and in many cases even provide legitimacy by themselves, they also serve to erode legitimacy under certain circumstances. Moreover, strategic relationships often betray true national motivations and interests, particularly when those engagements appear to contradict national rhetoric and values. In turn, this inflicts collateral damage on legitimacy. Consequently, while American foreign policy largely dictates with whom we form alliances, ostensibly in line with our national interests and commensurate with our national morals, U.S. military commanders and planners must account for the influences and

---

[17]Falk, Juergensmeyer, and Popovski, eds., *Legality and Legitimacy in Global Affairs*, 57.

[18]Ibid., 64.

effects—whether real or perceived—that contentious alliances have on the U.S. military's legitimacy.

Assumptions

There are a number of assumptions to address before proceeding further. First, this discussion assumes legitimacy is not merely a principle of joint operations but also a core component of American war strategy. Second, it assumes the United States pursues and secures its alliances at the discretion of civilian foreign policymakers. Consequently, alliances are a core characteristic of the American framework of war, relied upon for access and resource needs, and leveraged as a source of authority to confer legitimacy itself. Third, it assumes the U.S. military seeks an operational approach that best serves its own interests despite frequent employment as a benevolent hegemon or as part of a multilateral coalition. Specifically, its interests entail maximizing its operational efficiency and preserving its forces while minimizing its risk.[19] Fourth, it assumes legitimacy not only exists, but that the U.S. military is capable of securing it on an intercultural basis and, in turn, able to leverage it for maximum operational benefit to achieve mission and overall strategic objectives. Fifth and final, the entire premise of this discussion hinges on the assumption that the international community—an international society— exists, consciously linked by common or overlapping interests and values and, in turn, "bound by a common set of rules."[20] In the absence of such a community, the concept of legitimacy has no relevance and the conventional notion behind alliances has no purchase.[21]

---

[19]Hurd, "Legitimacy and Authority in International Politics," 396.

[20]Ian Clark, *Legitimacy in International Society* (New York: Oxford University Press, 2005), 6.

[21]Ibid., 5.

LEGITIMACY

Legitimacy is arguably one of the most important components of modern warfare for the U.S. military, doctrinally reinforced as one of its core operating principles and increasingly invoked to justify its operations abroad and world politics writ large.[22] Indeed, concerns over legitimacy pervade nearly every aspect of international relations, especially when relations sour and result in military conflict. Yet, it is simultaneously one of the most ill understood components of contemporary operations. The meaning and significance of legitimacy remains an "elusive and understudied" concept among scholars.[23] Specifically, considerable ambiguities emerge when the focus of legitimacy turns to "its delineation, its source, and its importance."[24] This presents quite a challenge for U.S. military commanders and planners attempting to navigate the modern operational environment, particularly amidst a near-compulsory framework of alliances and strategic partnerships. For something so readily invoked to justify the use of military force, let alone a cornerstone principle repeatedly referenced in the U.S. military's doctrine, it is vitally important to gain greater understanding of legitimacy before assessing the role that alliances play in either fortifying or eroding it.

Several aspects of legitimacy require further discussion. First, one must frame legitimacy as a subset of power, not only as a "currency of power" but also as an alternative to coercive or persuasive measures of military influence often used to secure compliance.[25] Second, one must identify the types or sources of legitimating authority in order to inform U.S. military efforts to

---

[22]Falk, Juergensmeyer, and Popovski, eds., *Legality and Legitimacy in Global Affairs*, 15.

[23]G. John Ikenberry, review of *Legitimacy in International Society*, by Ian Clark, *Foreign Affairs* 84, no. 5 (Sep/Oct 2005): 168.

[24]Ibid.

[25]Hurd, "Legitimacy and Authority in International Politics," 379.

design operational approaches that uphold and reinforce legitimacy while adequately leveraging the benefits of alliances, especially when alliances present a means of bolstering legitimacy. Third, any discussion of legitimacy must address the notions of consensus and compliance, both of which are fundamental components and goals of legitimacy. Finally, the role of perception must be discussed, in part because it plays such an integral role in the mere existence of legitimacy but also because it represents a significant factor for military planners and commanders to consider when developing an operational approach and corresponding narrative. Indeed, military actions may in fact be morally or legally justifiable; however, they are not legitimate unless they are perceived as such.[26] In order to establish a baseline understanding for further discussion of legitimacy, one must define the term and identify the various causes for its conceptual obscurity, particularly for members of the U.S. military.

Legitimacy Defined

The definition of legitimacy largely depends on the context of its use. In the context of international relations, it refers to "the belief by an actor that a rule or institution ought to be obeyed."[27] This, of course, leaves plenty of room for further contextual interpretation, particularly because beliefs are so subjective and far from universal. Narrowing in on a more refined definition that acknowledges the expected variations in legitimacy according to disparate context and cultural backgrounds yields the following definition: "Legitimacy is a generalized perception or assumption that the actions of an entity are desirable, proper, or appropriate within some

---

[26]Christian Reus-Smit, "International Crises of Legitimacy," *International Politics* 44, no. 2-3 (2007): 159.

[27]Ian Hurd, *After Anarchy: Legitimacy and Power in the United Nations Security Council* (Princeton: Princeton University Press, 2007), 30.

11

socially constructed system of norms, values, beliefs, and definitions."[28] Making this definition relevant and applicable in the context of military operations requires only the recognition that the military is the "entity" it references. However, this definition still suggests a number of points that need further clarification, namely the points that legitimacy derives from some semblance of socially constructed authority, that it depends largely on perception, and that such perception is generalized implying some measure of consent, whether implicit or explicit. Finally, there seems to be a recurring theme among all conceptions of legitimacy: social perception and recognition.[29] This alone distinguishes legitimacy from any of the values whence it derives, namely the values of "rationality, justice, legality, and morality."[30] Indeed, the critical factor that differentiates legitimacy from these aforementioned values is the need for social recognition.[31]

Causes behind the Conceptual Obscurity of Legitimacy

There are a number of reasons why legitimacy is such an ill-understood and often contentious concept, particularly when justifying the use of military force. For one, there are not many historical precedents of legitimacy being a significant precondition to war or a noteworthy factor influencing its conduct. Legitimacy has certainly not been a significant concern for American military commanders, not to the extent that victory has consumed their thoughts. Indeed, military commanders have long been more concerned with winning wars—as they should—than in being justified to conduct wars. The U.S. military has typically been interested in legitimacy only to the extent its actions preserve whatever degree of legitimacy already exists.

---

[28]Mark C. Suchman, "Managing Legitimacy: Strategies and Institutional Approaches," *Academy of Management Review* 20, no. 3 (Jul 1995): 574.

[29]Falk, Juergensmeyer, and Popovski, eds., *Legality and Legitimacy in Global Affairs*, 75.

[30]Ibid.

[31]Reus-Smit, "International Crises of Legitimacy," 160.

This is no longer the case, particularly in an era when legitimacy may itself be the decisive factor in winning a war.[32] In the modern operational environment, legitimacy is paramount, in many cases supplanting law itself as justification for military action.[33] Reliance on legitimacy, especially by the United States, continues to increase as international laws fail to accommodate the complexities of the modern operational environment.[34] Furthermore, the invocation of legitimacy to justify the use of military force "more naturally encourages attention being given to questions of the *appropriate* authority to act coercively in a range of contested conditions without necessarily accepting or rejecting the primacy and relevance of law as the basis for assessment."[35] For a nation of laws like the United States, the concept of legitimacy provides a crucial source of justification to act militarily, especially when its actions may not be legally sanctioned. This highlights an interesting aspect of legitimacy: while often used to supplant law as the source of authority to justify military actions abroad, law is itself a source of authority from which legitimacy derives, a point to be discussed in more detail shortly. Nonetheless, this just highlights why the concept of legitimacy remains so ill understood.

Another reason why legitimacy in the context of military operations seems so obscure is that it (the concept of legitimacy) has been traditionally limited to academic discussions of international relations (IR) and social science theories. Among such discussions, legitimacy takes

---

[32]U.S. Department of Defense, Joint Chiefs of Staff, *JP 3-0, Joint Operations*, A-4.

[33]Janne Haaland Matlary, "The Legitimacy of Military Intervention: How Important Is a Un Mandate?" *Journal of Military Ethics* 3, no. 2 (2004): 135. The NATO-led Kosovo-intervention of 1999 represents a classic contemporary example where military action was considered legitimate on moral grounds—a necessary humanitarian mission—but lacked the legal backing of a UN mandate. This illustrates that legal legitimacy is necessary and desirable, but not always sufficient to warrant and justify military action.

[34]Falk, Juergensmeyer, and Popovski, eds., *Legality and Legitimacy in Global Affairs*, 6.

[35]Ibid., 15.

on a characterization of being "an intangible factor" with "great practical experience."[36]

Furthermore, there exist extreme views of legitimacy within those discussions that question its mere existence, maintaining it is a socially constructed reality, one based largely on perception, and represents nothing more than a cleverly fabricated rationale to justify controversial actions.[37] Nevertheless, no modern military—American or otherwise—can discount the integral role legitimacy now plays in achieving victory. In fact, modern wars are often contingent on a legitimating resolution or declaration from a recognized source of authority like the United Nations (UN) or U.S. Congress. Once conferred, the U.S. military in particular goes to staggering lengths—implementing policies of restraint and imposing strict rules of engagement on its own forces—to forestall any loss of legitimacy. Therefore, while the concept may be obscure, the importance of legitimacy is quite clear to the U.S. military.

Perhaps the most common reason for the ambiguous nature of legitimacy as it relates to the use of military force—and certainly the cause of its contentious nature—involves the "practice of legitimation" and the consensus required to confer legitimacy.[38] The practice of legitimation refers to the process of mediating consensus. However, the very consensus that this process yields requires legitimacy itself. In other words, consensus is both the source of legitimacy as well as a possible effect and outcome of it.[39] Furthermore, there are vastly different perspectives and priorities among members of the international community that serve to modulate the degree of achievable consensus. This begs the question: if legitimacy depends on developing

---

[36] Robert Kagan, "Looking for Legitimacy in All the Wrong Places," *Foreign Policy* no. 137 (Jul/Aug 2003): 70.

[37] Adele Santana, "Three Elements of Stakeholder Legitimacy," *Journal of Business Ethics* 105, no. 2 (2012): 257–65.

[38] Clark, *Legitimacy in International Society*, 4.

[39] Ibid., 206.

a broad consensus among members of the international community, then how broad is broad enough and who decides that metric?[40] The answer to that question is quite subjective, as evidenced by the acrimonius debates that often occur within international legitimating bodies like the UN Security Council, and is therefore the reason why legitimacy remains such a contentious subject.[41]

Indeed, there are plenty of reasons why legitimacy remains so elusive—both in concept and in practice. However, that does not relieve U.S. military planners and commanders from their responsibility to fully consider legitimacy when developing an operational approach. On the contrary, it only highlights the challenge they face in navigating the modern operational environment. Furthermore, navigating that environment within a framework of policy-dictated alliances further exacerbates the problem of developing consensus, particularly when trying to adequately represent a greater and more diverse spread of national interests in the process. At a minimum, it emphasizes the importance of nesting the military's operational approach within the overarching strategic guidance communicated internationally through foreign policy rhetoric. Failure to do so risks creating a perception of mismatch between America's words and deeds. When perceived military actions fail to match the stated intentions and policy rhetoric that preceded such actions, suspicions among the international community arise. Suspicions foment mistrust, which, in turn, hinders the process of gaining the international consensus necessary to legitimate military action. The U.S. military must be extra cognizant of this dynamic when planning and conducting military operations abroad for two main reasons. First, there are significant operational ramifications of stoking anti-hegemonic fears throughout the international

---

[40]Robert Kagan, "America's Crisis of Legitimacy," *Foreign Affairs* 83, no. 2 (Mar/Apr 2004): 82.

[41]Clark, *Legitimacy in International Society*, 28.

community. Such fears may thwart legitimacy and incite anti-American sentiment and violence, thereby complicating military operations abroad. Second, if military actions contradict diplomatic rhetoric, then they undermine the credibility and legitimacy of both—America's diplomacy and its military. The U.S. military can ill afford that effect. Instead, it must make every effort to plan and conduct military actions that reinforce the credibility of America's commitment to "operate within an institutionalized political order" and encourage the consensus needed to beget legitimacy.[42]

Legitimacy as a Currency of Power

As previously noted, there exists an inextricable link between power and legitimacy. Some scholars suggest power and legitimacy are distinct social phenomena, defining power in terms of "material might" and legitimacy as a "valuable addendum to power" that makes power more socially acceptable.[43] Under this construct, legitimacy is not a source of power; rather, it is "treated as a veil or mantle that disguises the true nature of power, making it appear more palatable, less offensive or brutal than it might otherwise."[44] This perspective of the power-legitimacy relationship suggests power in the absence of legitimacy is not only feasible but also socially unconstrained. It is the sort of power commonly characterized by material capabilities like money and guns.[45] More specifically for the expected readers of this monograph, it is the sort of power characterized by military force and military-wielded capabilities like nuclear and

---

[42]G. John Ikenberry, "Institutions, Strategic Restraint, and the Persistence of American Postwar Order," *International Security* 23, no. 3 (Winter 1998/99): 65.

[43]Reus-Smit, "International Crises of Legitimacy," 160.

[44]Ibid., 161.

[45]Ibid., 162.

conventional weapons.[46] However, one cannot propagate this view without inviting considerable ridicule, especially in the modern operational environment.[47]

Indeed, the contrasting view of the power-legitimacy relationship holds the two as inseparable, suggesting power without legitimacy is impotent and more costly while legitimacy without power is largely irrelevant.[48] German sociologist Max Weber defined power as "a person's ability to impose his will upon others despite resistance."[49] More recently, Joseph Nye described power as "the ability to effect the outcomes you want, and if necessary, to change the behavior of others to make this happen."[50] Neither definition restricts power to material capabilities. On the contrary, they support the contemporary notion that power may include non-material factors as well. These factors include "ideas, beliefs, norms, and rules" and the "institutional structures and communicative processes that embed and mobilize them" like the practice of legitimation and the process of mediating consent.[51] In defining power, Weber further distinguishes two basic types of power: the type that rests on the ability to influence one's interests through coercion or persuasion, and the type that rests on legitimate authority (Appendix

---

[46]Alexander Wendt, *Social Theory of International Politics* (Cambridge: Cambridge University Press, 1999), 92.

[47]The author defines the 'modern operational environment' as that which emerged after the end of the Cold War.

[48]"Legitimacy cannot be divorced from power. Legitimacy constrains power, while also being an important element of it. Power also impacts upon the practice of legitimacy, and contributes to the substance of the principles of legitimacy that come to be accepted. It is, in any case, only within the context of power relations that legitimacy becomes relevant at all." Clark, *Legitimacy in International Society*, 20.

[49]Peter M. Blau, "Critical Remarks on Weber's Theory of Authority," *American Political Science Review* 57, no. 2 (June 1963): 306.

[50]Joseph S. Nye Jr., *The Paradox of American Power: Why the World's Only Superpower Can't Go It Alone* (New York: Oxford University Press, 2003), 4.

[51]Reus-Smit, "International Crises of Legitimacy," 162.

A).[52] The true delineation between the two comes down to compliance and the degree of effort necessary to achieve such compliance, a topic addressed in more detail shortly. Suffice it to say, however, that among the three primary currencies of power (namely, coercion, self-interest, and legitimacy, all of which will be discussed further in reference to their ability to achieve compliance), legitimate power is the preferable currency with which the U.S. military should 'purchase' or achieve its operational objectives.[53] Recent U.S. military engagements abroad only serve to reinforce this notion as they highlight the inherent limits to the operational results that coercive military measures produce.[54]

By this point, the importance of legitimacy should be growing more lucid. This is not to suggest its importance was ever in question, only that it is greatly underestimated in the role it can and should play for U.S. military planners and commanders charged with navigating today's operational environment. Considering how pivotal legitimacy is to the nature and conduct of modern military operations, the U.S. military must have a more thorough understanding of the concept and, more specifically, the sources of authority from which it derives.

Sources of Legitimating Authority

Max Weber was arguably one of the first theorists to systematically dismantle and analyze the concept of legitimacy. In doing so, Weber identified three primary types of legitimating authority: legal, traditional, and charismatic.[55] While each was unlikely to be found

---

[52]Blau, "Critical Remarks on Weber's Theory of Authority," 306.

[53]Hurd, "Legitimacy and Authority in International Politics," 379.

[54]The author contends that the military operations of the past decade in Iraq and Afghanistan reinforced conventional notions held by the U.S. military their operational objectives can rarely be achieved through material measures of power alone.

[55]Max Weber, *The Theory of Social and Economic Organization*, ed. Talcott Parsons, trans. A.M. Henderson and Talcott Parsons (New York: Oxford University Press, 1947), 328.

in its pure and isolated form in specific historic cases, Weber argued the analysis of each

individually was crucial to understanding their roles collectively when grappling with this

complicated notion of legitimacy. He ultimately suggested, however, that a consortium-like

synthesis of these authorities typically confers legitimacy, and lasting legitimacy at that.[56]

Legal authority (also called legal-rational authority) derives from what Weber called

"rational grounds" whereby the normative rules and those in a position of authority under such

rules establish the legality of orders or actions.[57] It is predicated on a belief in the "supremacy of

the law whatever its specific content" and based on the core assumption that "a body of legal

rules has been deliberately established to further the rational pursuit of collective goals."[58] Most

Western governments and internationally recognized institutions like the UN represent sources of

legal authority, derived explicitly from the domestic constitutional writs and international laws by

which they govern and through which they assert power and influence. The effectiveness of legal

authority largely depends on the acceptance of its validity.[59]

Traditional authority stems from what Weber described as "immemorial traditions and

the legitimacy of the status of those exercising authority under them."[60] In other words, it is

authority rooted in historical precedents and long-standing social mores. Examples of traditional

authority range from hereditary monarchies (i.e. noble lineage) to divinity (e.g. priests and kings)

---

[56]Weber, *The Theory of Social and Economic Organization*, 329.

[57]Ibid., 328.

[58]Blau, "Critical Remarks on Weber's Theory of Authority," 308.

[59]Weber, *The Theory of Social and Economic Organization*, 329.

[60]Ibid., 328.

to simple gerontocracy (i.e. rule by the elders).[61] The effectiveness of traditional authority

depends on loyalty and adherence to those "immemorial traditions" described by Weber.[62]

Finally, Weber explains that charismatic authority relies on "devotion to the specific and

exceptional sanctity, heroism or exemplary character of an individual person, and of the

normative patterns or order revealed or ordained by him."[63] Personality dictates the degree of this

authority whereby the stronger the personality, the more pronounced and durable that authority.

Furthermore, charismatic authority is likely to elicit strong passions among followers, even

sparking radicalism under the right conditions.[64] However, charismatic authority is often

susceptible to swift discredit under the wrong conditions, particularly when charismatic authority

alone is insufficient to confer legitimacy upon action.[65] Weber further explains charisma as that

"quality of an individual personality by virtue of which he is set apart from ordinary men and

treated as endowed with supernatural, superhuman, or at least specifically exceptional powers or

qualities."[66] National and military leaders often exhibit charismatic authority throughout history,

regardless of whether they are famous or infamous. Napoleon famously illustrated charismatic

authority at the turn of the nineteenth century as he led the French *Grande Armée* to a number of

decisive victories in Europe. Conversely, infamous national leaders such as Adolph Hitler and

Joseph Stalin relied heavily on charismatic authority to command their armies and control their

people. Moreover, as history adjudicates the legacies of each, it becomes readily apparent that

---

[61]Weber, *The Theory of Social and Economic Organization*, 346.

[62]Ibid., 341.

[63]Ibid., 328.

[64]Ibid., 359.

[65]Ibid., 360.

[66]Ibid., 358.

charismatic authority may be the most memorable but also the most precarious, particular in the context of legitimating specific military or militant actions. The efficacy of charismatic authority relies entirely on the trust and belief of those under such authority.[67]

Moral authority is one type of authority that escapes Weber's aforementioned analysis and discussion. As a basis of legitimacy, moral authority is undoubtedly a recurring theme underlying modern military actions, particularly those conducted by the United States. Specifically, the United States often uses moral authority to justify military action that lacks broad consensus, and invokes it in the perceived absence of all other sources of legitimacy. Moral authority encompasses the "fundamental assumptions that guide our perceptions of the world."[68] It is authority derived from a common understanding of right versus wrong, and a corresponding willingness to uphold 'right' and oppose 'wrong' in a culturally diverse world that does not always agree on the delineation between the two. Indeed, moral authority is firmly rooted in the belief that there are certain immutable rights and universally accepted moral principles, the defenses of which constitute moral imperatives and legitimize military actions. Of course, it is an exceedingly difficult task to identify those universal morals and principles due to the cultural disparity of values and moral interpretations in the world. This challenge only reinforces the notion argued by leading sociologists Peter Berger and Thomas Luckmann who claimed concepts like legitimacy and moral authority represented socially constructed knowledge. They argued that society crafts a cultural reality and corresponding body of knowledge out of necessity and for survival. As such, the body of knowledge wherein 'legitimacy' and 'moral authority' exist represented "the sum total of 'what everybody knows' about a social world, an assemblage of

---

[67]Weber, *The Theory of Social and Economic Organization*, 359.

[68]James Davison Hunter, *Culture Wars: The Struggle to Control the Family, Art, Education, Law, and Politics in America*, Reprint ed. (New York: Basic Books, 1992), 119.

maxims, morals, proverbial nuggets of wisdom, values and beliefs, myths, and so forth…such knowledge constitutes the motivating dynamics of institutionalized conduct."[69] Over time, these social constructions evolve into societal norms, institutional guidelines that define moral behavior, frame moral authority, and ultimately confer legitimacy.

Despite this seemingly fatalistic conclusion derived from Berger and Luckmann's existential interrogative, their argument actually supports not only the existence of these specific concepts (legitimacy and moral authority) but also the existence of institutionalized universalities. Life, liberty, and security of person represent just such universalities and globally recognized rights that, in turn, serve as core justifications for military action on moral grounds.[70] Counterterrorism and counter-genocide military operations are two modern missions that invoke moral authority as the source of their legitimacy. The indiscriminate killing of innocent civilians is a morally repugnant and reprehensible violation of man's immutable right to life. This is a universally accepted moral stance and, in turn, sufficient to legitimize retaliatory military action or unsanctioned humanitarian missions. The recent U.S. military operations in Iraq and Afghanistan and the earlier North Atlantic Treaty Organization (NATO) intervention in Kosovo serve as contemporary examples whereby the lead agent invoked its moral authority to curb mass atrocity, prevent the regional proliferation of WMD, and combat terrorism. More recently, the UN Security Council invoked the controversial concept of Responsibility to Protect (R2P) to justify military action against the Muammar al-Qaddafi regime in Libya. The resulting UN Security Council Resolution (UNSCR) 1973 established the legal authority to commence such

---

[69]Peter L. Berger and Thomas Luckmann, *The Social Construction of Reality: A Treatise in the Sociology of Knowledge* (Garden City, NY: Doubleday, 1966), 65.

[70]United Nations, "The Universal Declaration of Human Rights," under "Article 3," http://www.un.org/en/documents/udhr/index.shtml (accessed January 1, 2013).

action.[71] In effect, the UN Security Council co-opted its moral authority with its legal authority to establish the legitimacy of its eventual military actions. It based its action on the internationally accepted legal principle of *jus cogens*, Latin for 'compelling law' and better known in English as a peremptory norm, which characterizes and identifies timeless and universally-recognized norms.[72] International crimes that violate *jus cogens* include "aggression, genocide, crimes against humanity, war crimes, piracy, slavery and slave-related practices, and torture."[73] Moral conduct is a key prerequisite to invoking moral authority. The old adage "actions speak louder than words" is certainly applicable in this sense. Consequently, it is imperative that U.S. actions consistently exhibit and support moral behavior else its moral authority and ability to invoke it when justifying military actions may be lost. This is precisely the dilemma the United States faces when it engages in partnerships with nations whose actions demonstrate immorality and in many cases violate peremptory norms. In doing so, the United States subordinates its morality to its interests and, in effect, commits fratricide on its moral authority.

An additional type of authority neither addressed by Weber nor derived from any of the aforementioned sources of authority is the sort of power and influence that springs from collectivism, typically manifested in the form of multilateral consensus. Alliances are a long-standing venue in which its constituents, by their collective agreement, represent the sort of authority necessary to render military actions legitimate. Max Weber did not address this type of

---

[71]Jayshree Bajoria, "Libya and the Responsibility to Protect," *Council on Foreign Relations Analysis Brief* (March 24, 2011): under "first paragraph,", http://www.cfr.org/libya/libya-responsibility-protect/p24480 (accessed November 23, 2012).

[72]Falk, Juergensmeyer, and Popovski, eds., *Legality and Legitimacy in Global Affairs*, 436.

[73]M. Cherif Bassiouni, "International Crimes," *Law and Contemporary Problems* 59, no. 4 (Autumn 1996): 68.

authority, presumably because the individual cannot exercise it; he examined authority only as it relates to the individual. This does not repudiate collectivism as a source of authority from which to extract legitimacy. However, it is a risky and certainly controversial basis upon which to claim legitimacy, primarily because there is no objective metric to gauge what qualifies as sufficient collective consensus. It is precisely the sort of collectivism demonstrated by both sides—Axis and Allied—during World War II. Both claimed their actions were legitimate based on collective interests and member status in their respective alliances, yet history may arbitrate those claims of legitimacy as they stack up morally or legally. The main point here is that an alliance qualifies as viable source of authority to establish legitimacy.

The Roles of Consensus and Compliance in Legitimacy

The aforementioned claim that consensus and compliance are integral elements of legitimacy warrants further discussion.[74] Consensus is fundamental to legitimacy as a measure of social cohesion and sufficient agreement among diverse members of the international community and their corresponding disparate interests.[75] This sort of consensus serves to sanction military action. It need not be unanimous, but should represent a "willing acceptance of what is the subject of consensus."[76] Ironically, this is precisely where the notion of consensus becomes problematic. The degree of consensus required to legitimate military action is highly subjective and contextual. One need only look back a few decades to cite specific examples like the NATO-led intervention in Kosovo in 1999 or the U.S. invasion of Iraq in 2003 where the legitimacy of military action was highly contested. As mentioned earlier, there is no objective metric to determine the degree

---

[74]The author suggests consensus is a precursor to and product of legitimacy, while compliance is a desirable consequence of legitimacy.

[75]Clark, *Legitimacy in International Society*, 164.

[76]P. H. Partridge, *Consent and Consensus* (London: Pall Mall Press, 1971), 17.

of agreement required to qualify as 'consensus' and, in turn, confer legitimacy. Some also suggest that voluntary consensus is a false description in an international community shadowed by American hegemony. That is, "consensus is suffused with power relations, and it is hard to see where coercion stops and voluntarism starts in the production of it...consensus can be encouraged, and thwarted, by a range of power-political, self-interested, and coercive means."[77] In other words, the shear might of the U.S. military pressures other members of the international community to concede to the social pressure exerted by America's interest-based pursuits. While this may or may not be an accurate representation of consensus in the modern operational environment, it highlights a perception for the U.S. military to consider when planning and conducting operations abroad.

Compliance is the ultimate goal (or output) of power, and legitimacy makes such compliance far less costly to achieve and far more consistent over the long term (Appendix A). Henry Kissinger described the relationship between power and legitimacy in his seminal work *Diplomacy* as mutually dependent, saying "Power without legitimacy tempts tests of strength; legitimacy without power tempts empty posturing."[78] Indeed, legitimacy gives power greater depth and durability. However, legitimacy represents just one currency of power. According to Ian Hurd, the other currencies of power include coercion and self-interest.[79] To understand these, consider the following three reasons why an actor might comply with a rule: (1) the actor fears the punishment of rule enforcers for not complying, (2) the actor views compliance with the rule as in its own self-interest, and (3) the actor feels the rule is inherently legitimate and ought to be

---

[77]Clark, *Legitimacy in International Society*, 163, 192.

[78]Henry A. Kissinger, *Diplomacy* (New York: Simon & Schuster, 1994), 77.

[79]Hurd, "Legitimacy and Authority in International Politics," 379.

obeyed.[80] In each case, compliance is the result but for significantly different reasons and at considerably different cost to the enforcer.

In the first case, the actual or threatened use of coercive measures yields compliance, albeit very costly, weak at its core, and counterproductive in the long run.[81] According to Hurd, coercion refers to "a relation of asymmetrical physical power among agents, where this asymmetry is applied to [change] the behavior of the weaker agent."[82] He further explains that the operative mechanism in coercion is fear or "simple compellance," where fear of being punished by a stronger power produces acquiescence.[83] This is precisely the sort of compliance that Thucydides once highlighted in the exchange between the Athenians and the Melians in 416 BC. Compliance based on coercion comes at a price though, literally. Coercive measures require significant expenditures in resources and manpower, ranging from near-term costs of initial enforcement to long-term costs of sustained surveillance to detect lapses of compliance. It also yields a very shallow degree of compliance, where the actors cease to comply when the enforcing agent either departs or is simply not looking.[84] Worst of all, especially for sustained military operations, compliance achieved through coercion precipitates "resentments that can fuel the flames of opposition."[85] While coercion may be the simplest and most expeditious means to achieve compliance, it is highly inefficient and often creates more adversity in the end.

---

[80]Hurd, "Legitimacy and Authority in International Politics," 379.

[81]Ikenberry, *After Victory*, 53.

[82]Hurd, "Legitimacy and Authority in International Politics," 383.

[83]Ibid.

[84]Ibid., 384.

[85]Ikenberry, *After Victory*, 54.

In the second case, compliance is the product of persuasive measures that stress it is in the actor's self-interest to comply. Such compliance is neither the sole result of the more dominant enforcer's persuasive incentives nor the result of the actor's intrinsic motivation to seek what best serves self-interest. It is the type of compliance achieved only after a rigorous cost-benefit analysis within the mind of the actor. Furthermore, while the actor weighs the costs and benefits of compliance, the actor remains cognizant of the enforcer's capacity to transition from positive to negative incentives. Margaret Levi refers to this dynamic as quasi-voluntary compliance: the compliance is voluntary to the extent the actors choose to comply, but it is quasi-voluntary because the actors will be punished if they do not comply and are caught.[86] In many ways, compliance based on self-interest is not much different than compliance based on coercion; indeed, they both are forms of utilitarianism where the consequences of noncompliance weigh heavily in the final decision to comply.[87] Like coercion, this type of compliance comes at a price. First, continued compliance is often contingent on a continued "stream of benefits" and incentives from the enforcer, and the actors are "constantly recalculating the expected payoff" of remaining compliant or being noncompliant if the latter offers greater utility.[88] Second, loyal relationships are difficult to maintain because "actors do not value the relation itself, only the benefits accruing from it."[89] Indeed, this type of compliance represents a costly and precarious basis upon which to rely when conducting long-term military operations.

---

[86]Margaret Levi, *Of Rule and Revenue* (Berkeley: University of California Press, 1988), 32.

[87]Desmond P. Ellis, "The Hobbesian Problem of Order: A Critical Appraisal of the Normative Solution," *American Sociological Review* 36, no. 4 (Aug 1971): 693.

[88]Hurd, "Legitimacy and Authority in International Politics," 387.

[89]Ibid.

Finally, in the third case, compliance is the result of the actor's genuine belief that it is both right and necessary to comply. According to Hurd, "the operative process in legitimation is the internalization by the actor of an external standard…when the actor's sense of its own interests is partly constituted by a force outside itself, that is, by the standards, laws, rules, and norms present in the community, existing at the intersubjective level."[90] Quite simply, compliance becomes a matter of duty for the actor, driven by an internal sense of moral obligation. For U.S. military operations abroad, early and lasting compliance—particularly the type that derives from intrinsic motivations among the host (or target) nation—is certainly the preferred context in which to operate. Consequently, the more the U.S. military does to secure legitimacy in advance of such operations, the less costly it will theoretically be for it in the end.

The fundamental components of legitimacy are numerous and significant, representing no small hurdles to overcome when trying to secure and maintain legitimacy. While sometimes underestimated and often ill understood, its role in U.S. military operations is unmistakable. Legitimacy fulfills the modern prerequisite that the international community sanction military action, thereby preserving access to the aggregate resources and influence the international community provides. Without the legitimacy that stems from operating through an international consensus, the U.S. military risks facing growing hostility around the world, no matter its cause.[91] It also serves as a force multiplier for military operations by conserving combat power for operational tasks other than the costs associated with enforcing, securing, and maintaining compliance. Legitimacy begets low levels of opposition and thereby reduces the costs of coercive

---

[90]Hurd, "Legitimacy and Authority in International Politics," 388.

[91]Fareed Zakaria, "Our Way: The Trouble with Being the World's Only Superpower," *New Yorker* 78, no. 31 (Oct 14 & 21, 2002): 81.

or persuasive measures to achieve compliance.[92] Nevertheless, legitimacy is a function of the context and conditions of each unique situation. Above all, the realization of actual legitimacy is a function of the prevailing perception of legitimacy, or lack thereof. Consequently, the U.S. military must ensure it conducts operations concomitant with long-term preservation of this key enabler.

The Role of Perception in Legitimacy

As mentioned earlier, the single common denominator for legitimacy is perception. Berger and Luckmann described perception as "an ongoing correspondence" between competing realities shaped by disparate perspectives.[93] Others have likened it to the common cliché about beauty, suggesting legitimacy "resides in the eyes of the beholder."[94] Perhaps it is simple enough to say that when it comes to legitimacy, perception is reality. Therefore, any military action, regardless of its nature or intent, lacks legitimacy if the perceived authority used to justify, sanction, or authorize such action lacks legitimacy. Furthermore, according to IR professor Christian Reus-Smit, "No action can be coherently described as legitimate if it is not socially recognized as rightful."[95] This highlights vulnerabilities for the U.S. military in trying to preserve its own legitimacy, describing what amounts to an impossible task to ensure its legitimacy is socially recognized let alone recognized as rightful. However, it also highlights opportunities for the military to exploit, namely the opportunity to use public narrative or overt action to influence perceptions of an adversary's legitimacy. For example, one of the primary ways the United States

---

[92]Reus-Smit, "International Crises of Legitimacy," 164.

[93]Berger and Luckmann, *The Social Construction of Reality*, 23.

[94]B.E. Ashforth and B.W. Gibbs, "The Double-Edge of Organizational Legitimation," *Organization Science* 1, no. 2 (1990): 177.

[95]Reus-Smit, "International Crises of Legitimacy," 160.

seeks to marginalize terrorist organizations is to not only highlight their illegitimate methods of war on moral grounds but also call into question their legitimacy as an organization on legal and traditional grounds. In doing so, the United States publicly refutes terrorist attempts to invoke legal, traditional, and normative moral authority as a basis to legitimate their actions. According to Weber's theory, charismatic authority is the only remaining source of legitimacy for terrorists to claim. As previously mentioned, legitimacy founded solely on charismatic authority is precarious at best.

The primacy of perception greatly complicates efforts to secure and maintain legitimacy. Whenever legitimacy is in question, those who perceive it to be legitimate or illegitimate ultimately adjudicate the final answer. For the U.S. military, in particular, legitimacy signifies an endorsement of its actions by the international community, domestic community, or preferably both.[96] In the absence of perceived legitimacy, actual legitimacy theoretically does not exist. This is neither a sardonic admission of defeat nor a cynical suggestion that legitimacy is an irrelevant concept altogether. Rather, it illustrates how difficult legitimacy is to establish and how fragile it is to maintain.

Legitimacy as a U.S. Military Principle of Joint Operations

Legitimacy currently represents one of the twelve principles of joint operations for the U.S. military, considered a requisite component of its actions abroad.[97] It is a relatively new addition to its doctrine, but one that—along with restraint and perseverance—now defines how the U.S. military conducts its operations.[98] According to Joint Publication (JP) 3-0, the purpose of

---

[96]Bruce Gilley, "The Meaning and Measure of State Legitimacy: Results for 72 Countries," *European Journal of Political Research* 45, no. 3 (May 2006): 502.

[97]U.S. Department of Defense, Joint Chiefs of Staff, *JP 3-0, Joint Operations*, I-2.

[98]Ibid.

legitimacy is to "maintain legal and moral authority in the conduct of operations."[99] It also explains that legitimacy is "based on the actual and perceived legality, morality, and rightness of the actions from the various perspectives of interested audiences."[100] These statements are certainly correct, but as this monograph has explained thus far, there is far more to the art of establishing and sustaining military legitimacy. Consequently, a better understanding of what it is, who or what confers it, and how it affects military operations is crucial to aptly leverage the benefits it provides and avoid actions that may erode it.

Specifically for U.S. military commanders and planners, they must account for legitimacy—or the lack thereof—when developing their operational approach. They must make every effort to harness and exploit the force enabling and force multiplying effect of legitimacy, particular the byproduct of a more compliant operating environment. They must also carefully and deliberately construct the narrative and conduct actions in a manner that supports the perception of legitimacy. In the absence of actual or perceived legitimacy, they must be ready to dedicate additional resources and lines of effort to facilitate operations in an inhospitable operating environment. Quite simply, the U.S. military must be fully fluent in the language of legitimacy, both for its own operational good and for the good of America's strategic interests.

ALLIANCES

Not all alliances are equal. Some represent cohesion of common ideologies, others represent unified opposition to a mutual threat, and still others evolve from a combined pursuit of shared interests. Among those, there are formal alliances like NATO, which—like treaties—are the product of official ratification processes and outline explicit guidelines on member obligations

---

[99]U.S. Department of Defense, Joint Chiefs of Staff, *JP 3-0, Joint Operations*, A-4.

[100]Ibid.

31

for long-term objectives.[101] There are also informal alliances, more often characterized as ad hoc coalitions or strategic partnerships between nations for a limited purpose and duration.[102] Functionally, the difference between the two types is largely transparent, particularly in the role they play as a collective source of legitimating authority. To gain a greater understanding of alliances as a whole, this section will dig deeper into the delineation between formal and informal alliances and the corresponding ramifications of each type in the context of military operations. Additionally, it will also address the general motivations behind alliance formation, the purposes they presumably serve, and their role in conferring legitimacy. The intent here is not to outline every detail of alliances; quite simply, that level of detail is not necessary. Rather, the intent is to develop a more comprehensive understanding of alliances and the specific role they play in helping or hindering military legitimacy.

Whether formed to increase power or enhance security, alliances are the primary foreign policy means by which the military amplifies its combat capacity.[103] In most cases, alliances also serve as one of the primary mechanisms by which the military legitimates its actions abroad. In some situations, however, alliances are equally capable of eroding legitimacy. This latter aspect of alliances is precisely why the stakes are so high for U.S. military commanders and planners charged with walking this operational tightrope. Moreover, they must use extreme caution when designing and implementing operational approaches that heavily rely on alliances to succeed, particularly when legitimacy is critical to mission success.

---

[101]U.S. Department of Defense, Joint Chiefs of Staff, *JP 3-16, Multinational Operations* (Washington, DC: Government Printing Office, March 2007), I-1.

[102]Ibid.

[103]Dan Reiter, *Crucible of Beliefs: Learning, Alliances, and World Wars* (Ithaca: Cornell University Press, 1996), 41.

32

<u>Alliances Defined</u>

Alliances take on a number of forms, ostensibly driven by their intended purpose. Alliances shaped by cooperative security interests historically stem from a formal process by which stakeholders unite their collective capacity to counter a specific threat. As mentioned above, they are typically the result of a formal ratification process that outlines specific obligations and binding terms. The more traditional and formal definition holds,

> An alliance is a formal agreement among independent states to cooperate militarily. Alliances may include any variety of specific promises, but what they share in common is a written commitment to coordinated action in the event of crises with the potential to involve military conflict. Unlike tacit alignments, alliances begin, and often end, through active political choices. Not only do leaders agree to ally and sign a formal document indicating their allied status, but they [also] design the content of the agreement, specifying the actions they are obligated to take and the conditions under which they are obligated to take them.[104]

The formality of alliances is an important distinction because it indicates the degree to which participants are legally bound to abide by the terms of the alliance. Tacit alignments between or among nations functionally resemble formal alliances, but they fall well short of obligating stakeholders to specific and often limiting terms. Furthermore, formal alliances also serve as far better predictors of action because signatories and non-signatories alike know the specified conditions under which actions are both permitted and likely. As Dan Reiter, author of *Crucible of Beliefs: Learning, Alliances, and World Wars*, explains, formal alliances are "a very good indicator of the likelihood that one state will agree to defend another state if it is attacked."[105] Moreover, the binding nature of formal alliances pressures its members to fulfill its commitment to the alliance when called upon. For those nations that prefer to remain neutral members of the international community, the potential cost of this commitment does not outweigh the expected

---

[104]Brett Ashley Leeds and Burcu Savun, "Terminating Alliances: Why Do States Abrogate Agreements?" *Journal of Politics* 69, no. 4 (November 2007): 1119.

[105]Reiter, *Crucible of Beliefs*, 51.

benefit that alliances provide, namely increased security. As Reiter points out, "At the moment of truth in a military crisis, a formal alliance substantially increases the odds that an otherwise disinterested state will become involved because of the implications that breaking an alliance would have for that state's international reputation."[106] Perhaps most importantly, formal alliances establish a commonality between dissimilar cultures in the form of shared interests and mutual agreement. Consequently, they establish mutual legitimacy for the actions of each ally as long as those actions adhere to the terms of the alliance and do not violate *jus cogens*. This, however, raises the stakes for all alliance-seeking states that value legitimacy as a core principle underpinning their actions. If they unwisely form alliances with nations that behave immorally by international standards, then they run the risk of eroding their perceived moral authority. In other words, they are guilty by association, engaging in an interest-based alliance at the expense of their own long-term legitimacy. The collective and legal authority the alliance provides to legitimate military action may not offset the corresponding loss of moral authority, rendering overall legitimacy elusive or suspect at best.

A less rigid definition of an alliance asserts it is "a formal or informal arrangement for security cooperation between two or more sovereign states."[107] This definition bestows the title of 'alliance' on ad hoc partnerships like "coalitions of the willing" without the corresponding legal obligations associated with their more formal counterparts described above.[108] It is a liberal interpretation of alliances and allows far more freedom of maneuver in terms of adherence and application. This added versatility, however, creates tempting opportunities to betray the terms or

---

[106]Reiter, *Crucible of Beliefs*, 51.

[107]Stephen M. Walt, *The Origins of Alliance* (Ithaca: Cornell University Press, 1990), 12.

[108]Reese S. Rogers, "Alliances and Coalitions of the Willing: U.S. Legitimacy in Future Conflict" (master's thesis, U.S. Army War College, Carlisle Barracks, PA, 2010), 6.

intent of the alliance. A lack of formality effectively lessens the ramifications of violating the terms of the alliance. In other words, there is little or no incentive to remain loyal. Still, many states prefer the added flexibility—or put differently, the lack of constraint—informal relationships offer, which partly explains their growing favor in modern military operations.

For the United States in particular, reluctance to engage in binding alliances stretches back to its national origin during which the price of collaboration seemed to far outweigh the benefits. Its first exposure to the potential benefits of alliances came at a time when the United States had its hands full trying to secure its independence and garner national credibility; it could ill afford the added burden of alliance-driven obligations in foreign conflicts.[109] In fact, the American Founding Fathers punctuated this sentiment with their advice "to 'steer clear of permanent alliances,' avoid 'entangling alliances,' and to enter only into 'temporary alliances for extraordinary emergencies.'"[110] For a nation with a long-standing predilection for autonomy, informal alliances still seem to provide the best of both worlds: a means of advancing state interests without the obligatory encumbrances. In short, the potential rewards outweigh the probable risks, or so it would seem.

In all, the difference between formal and informal alliances boils down to reliability. Formal alliances are theoretically more reliable because they obligate their members and codify the agreement in writing. Informal alliances, while more convenient to form and ostensibly more flexible in function, do not have the capacity to hold their members accountable for their alliance commitments. Many alliance scholars suggest alliances—whether formal or informal—are only reliable to the extent the commitment costs of membership are not too high and the cooperative

---

[109]George C. Herring, *From Colony to Superpower: U.S. Foreign Relations Since 1776* (New York: Oxford University Press, 2008), 83.

[110]Sherwood-Randall, *Alliances and American National Security*, 4.

agreement continues to serve constituent interests.[111] Nevertheless, the delineation is an important one for U.S. military commanders and planners trying to leverage the benefits of alliances when developing operational approaches. Specifically, formal alliances offer a greater degree of organizational maturity as well as greater predictability and dependability. In turn, they offer a greater level of commonality that streamlines military operations.[112] More importantly, they mitigate the risk that coalition partners will abrogate their alliance commitments and thereby undercut U.S. military operations that depend on allied support.[113]

Drivers of Alliance Formation

Alliance formation draws upon numerous motivations that span the spectrum of national interests, ranging from security concerns to power ambitions. The fundamental drivers of alliance formation ultimately come down to a nation's degree of existing and desired power as well as its overarching national interests. In general terms, strong powers tend to pursue alliances for "geostrategic reasons such as bases and access to raw materials," and weak powers often possess "an important commodity or strategic location which the larger power values."[114] Conversely, weak powers tend to pursue alliances for internal reasons, not the least of which is to augment their own security. Of course, the strong powers—their strength measured largely by their military capacity in the context of alliances—possess the capacity to enhance the security of weak powers. In effect, this describes a dynamic whereby alliances serve the interests of both strong

---

[111]Brett Ashley Leeds, "Alliance Reliability in Times of War: Explaining State Decisions to Violate Treaties," *International Organization* 57, no. 4 (Autumn 2003): 802.

[112]U.S. Department of Defense, Joint Chiefs of Staff, *JP 3-16, Multinational Operations*, I-6.

[113]Leeds, "Alliance Reliability in Times of War," 803.

[114]John P. Miglietta, *American Alliance Policy in the Middle East, 1945-1992: Iran, Israel, and Saudi Arabia* (Lanham, MD: Lexington Books, 2002), 12, 14.

and weak powers alike. The strong powers gain the global access they desire by allying with weak powers; in turn, the weak powers benefit from the protective capacity of its stronger partner. In some cases, though, the access a strong power desires may also serve as a future means to bolster its security against a rising power and future threat. Such access enables global reach by the strong power to either engage the future threat directly or use a more indirect approach of containment or deterrence.

Most scholars and practitioners in the field of international relations view threats—real or perceived—as the primary drivers behind alliance formation, where the mere existence of threats signifies a linkage to national interests. In other words, a threat is not truly a threat unless it threatens a national interest. Furthermore, alliances "have no meaning apart from the adversary threat to which they are a response."[115] One of the most well known scholars on threat-centric alliance formation is Stephen M. Walt. In this seminal work *The Origins of Alliances*, he offers two primary strategies that states undertake when forming alliances to counter a significant external threat: balancing and bandwagoning.[116] Walt defines balancing as "allying with others against the prevailing threat" and bandwagoning as "alignment with the source of danger."[117] According to his theory, balancing is the preferred tendency because it enhances security by keeping the power of aggressor states in check. States jeopardize their very survival if they "fail to curb a potential hegemon before it becomes too strong."[118] They also maximize their influence in an alliance by joining the weaker side because the weaker side theoretically has a greater need

---

[115]Glenn H. Snyder, *Alliance Politics* (Ithaca: Cornell University Press, 2007), 192.

[116]Walt, *The Origins of Alliance*, 17.

[117]Ibid.

[118]Ibid., 18.

for external assistance in countering a threat.[119] In a bandwagoning approach, the weaker power may gain greater security because of the alliance but does not necessarily benefit from increased influence within the alliance.

Based on Walt's theory, this says one of three things about the prospects of America's alliances: (1) weaker nations will seek to ally with the United States in a bandwagoning approach to take advantage of its protective capacity, (2) the United States will seek to ally with weaker nations in order to gain access to scarce resources or impermissible regions, or (3) weaker nations, viewing American hegemony as a threat, will seek to ally with other U.S. adversaries in a balancing approach to keep America's power in check. An obvious question emerges from these alternatives, reminiscent of the way events played out for the Melians after the Athenians solicited their allegiance in the Melian Dialogue: if a strong state needs the resource or regional access held by a weak state and the weak state refuses to concede, what keeps the strong state from forcibly gaining access against the weaker state's will? The answer to this, particularly for the United States, points back to the dynamic that legitimacy plays in a nation's power. That is, to preserve lasting legitimacy and leverage it in the conduct of military operations abroad, the United States must not only operate within an alliance framework that, by itself, confers legitimacy via collective authority, but also solicit alliances that offer mutual benefit to its members. The United States can ill afford the repeated fall out that results from violating state sovereignty in order to achieve the access it needs or wants. Indeed, the best option is for the United States to pursue a sort of quid pro quo relationship in which there is an exchange of mutual benefits between the United States and its allies.

One final aspect to consider regarding the drivers of alliances is the expected duration of their utility and corresponding costs if maintained over the long run. Alex Wendt contends that

---

[119]Walt, *The Origins of Alliance*, 19.

alliances are "temporary coalitions of self-interested states who come together for instrumental reasons in response to a specific threat. Once the threat is gone, the coalition loses its rationale and should disband."[120] This is the predominant argument against the continued relevance and utility of the NATO alliance in modern military operations. The NATO alliance emerged, in part, as a Cold War mechanism for western powers to keep Soviet power in check, primarily by containing the global spread of its communist ideology.[121] According to Wendt's argument, when the Cold War ended and the Soviet threat effectively disappeared, NATO should have disbanded. However, instead of disbanding, the alliance actually adapted itself to address new threats and welcomed additional members in the process (Appendix B). Consequently, the value gained by continued employment through and with the NATO alliance, particularly with respect to its legitimating capacity, continues to motivate the United States to tend to this alliance.

One cannot say the same about the other partnerships America pursued and secured in the wake of the Cold War and, more specifically, those it secured as it embarked on its Global War on Terror in late 2001. Many of those strategic partnerships served America's immediate interests, namely to facilitate the U.S. military's global reach and access throughout the Middle East in order to conduct broad counterterrorism operations let alone two major combat operations in Afghanistan and Iraq. These relationships, however, came at a significant price, mostly in the form of monetary aid and foreign military sales (FMS) agreements (Appendix B). Suffice it to say that in the absence of a significant threat facing each of these respective partners, their incentive

---

[120]Alexander Wendt, "Collective Identity Formation and the International State," *American Political Science Review* 88, no. 2 (June 1994): 386.

[121]North Atlantic Treaty Organization, "A Short History of NATO," http://www.nato.int/history/nato-history.html (accessed February 24, 2013). According to NATO, the Soviet threat was only partially responsible for its formation. Its formation was driven by three main purposes: to deter Soviet expansionism, prevent the revival of nationalist militarism in Europe by keeping a strong North American presence on the continent, and to promote European political integration.

to remain partnered with the United States is contingent on such material benefit. In return, America gains continued or ready access to regions that facilitate its ongoing counterterrorism operations. In the meantime, some of these relationships do nothing to bolster U.S. military legitimacy. In particular, those strategic partners who are continually guilty of egregious moral indiscretion by international standards or who more recently supported America's adversaries certainly taint perceptions of U.S. legitimacy abroad.[122]

Alliances as a Basis for Legitimacy

Alliances, in fact, are most effective when their constituents have a stake in their durability and dependability. There is no better catalyst to forge long-term alliance commitment and resolve than "the shared recognition of common threats and a pledge to take action to counter them."[123] Furthermore, the key to constructing a durable and dependable alliance lies in its formality. That is, legitimate state representation must codify the pledge in writing and clearly articulate its terms and conditions. Incentives and disincentives alike must definitively reinforce commitment and discourage abrogation. The formal alliance serves this purpose most effectively. Despite an arduous and time-consuming process, especially in negotiating the consensus and developing the infrastructure in advance of its use, a formal alliance assures its stakeholders that it will fulfill its intended purpose as a viable security apparatus when necessary.

Leading alliance expert Dr. Elizabeth Sherwood-Randall insists legitimacy is a critical

---

[122]Joshua E. Keating, "America's Other Most Embarrassing Allies," *Foreign Policy* (January 31, 2011), under "Yemen," http://www.foreignpolicy.com/articles/2011/01/31/americas_other_most_embarrassing_allies (accessed February 9, 2013). Yemen currently serves U.S. interests by facilitating counterterrorism efforts, both inside Yemen and in the surrounding region. In 2011, FMS agreements with Yemen approached $1.4M. In 1990, Yemen's leadership at the time, Ali Abdullah Saleh, was a close ally of Saddam Hussein and supported Iraq's invasion of Kuwait, a military operation that drew U.S. military response in opposition.

[123]Wendt, "Collective Identity Formation and the International State," 2.

component of contemporary alliance policy and the basis for the "exercise of American power," particularly as the U.S. military navigates a very complex twenty-first century threat environment.[124] She cites three key events that significantly altered America's ability to exercise its power and greatly changed the rules of the alliance "game": the fall of the Berlin Wall on November 9, 1989 and subsequent collapse of the Soviet Union and Warsaw Pact; the terrorist attacks of September 11, 2001; and the U.S. initiation of preventive war in Iraq in March 2003, with a coalition of the willing in tow.[125] She suggests,

> With traditional approaches to prevention, deterrence, and defense under siege, alliances offer a crucial mechanism for working to achieve an updated consensus on when and how to use force. Planning for and using American power in a multinational context provides the single most effective mechanism for ensuring that U.S. actions are perceived to be legitimate. Acting without such international "cover" is increasingly problematic, because it foments resistance to U.S. policies and because the United States needs the help of others to achieve its goals, especially in the arduous and extended aftermath of most military operations. Acting through its alliances, the United States can blunt the hegemonic edge of American leadership, share costs and risks, and increase the prospects of success.[126]

Additionally, she contends U.S. alliances have a symbiotic effect on the credibility and legitimacy of its counterparts. "If America uses its power in ways that are perceived to respect international norms, it can bolster the global stature and influence of its allies."[127] In other words, the alliance framework provides a formal venue for the United States to demonstrate its trust and confidence in its alliance partners, thereby boosting their international influence. This has the cascading effect of engendering loyalty and commitment among partners who might otherwise oppose American objectives. In turn, their loyalty manifests itself in the form of greater acquiescence

---

[124]Sherwood-Randall, *Alliances and American National Security*, 10.

[125]Ibid., 14.

[126]Ibid.

[127]Ibid., 15.

with U.S.-oriented alliance agendas. Simply put, the United States reaps what it sows. By investing implicit approval in the alliance framework, the United States creates a more favorable environment in which to exploit the collective capacity of an alliance to advance its interests. Indeed, an American endorsement still goes a long way in the international community. It legitimizes the fundamental alliance apparatus and boosts the international standing of its partners. Consequently, the collective authority grounding American legitimacy remains both valid and durable, thereby serving as a reliable means to legitimate U.S. military operations abroad.

Interests or Ideologies as Bases for Alliances

One of the most enduring debates among IR theorists on the topic of alliances has to do with whether interests or ideologies shape and sustain alliance relationships. Most agree the two need not be mutually exclusive, but they are not equally represented among real world strategic partnerships. One of the better-known IR theorists to weigh in on this debate was famed realist Hans Morgenthau. He argued that states form alliances to "add to their own power the power of other nations, or…withhold the power of other nations from the adversary."[128] He further suggested expediency (i.e. self-interest) is the root driver of alliance formation, and that "a nation will shun alliances if it believes that it is strong enough to hold its own unaided or that the burden of the commitments resulting from the alliance is likely to outweigh the advantages to be expected."[129] This echoes the famous claim once made by the Prime Minister of England, Lord Palmerston, that nations have no permanent friends or enemies, only permanent interests.[130] It

---

[128]Hans J. Morgenthau, *Politics Among Nations: The Struggle for Power and Peace*, 4th ed. (New York: Knopf, 1967), 175.

[129]Ibid.

[130]Walt, *The Origins of Alliance*, 33.

also follows the logic once expressed by Thucydides that "identity of interests is the surest of bonds whether between states or individuals."[131] Morgenthau also suggested small states with relatively weak power capabilities still exert considerable influence in the international system if they possess key strategic resources or occupy "geostrategic geographical position."[132] Consequently, they represent considerable value to larger, more powerful states that require material or geographic access for advancing their particular national interests.

In general, this logic represents the supposition of this monograph regarding alliances, whether formal or informal: states will favor relationships that serve their interests long before they favor those that align with their ideology or moral foundation. These interests need not be the same or even similar; they only need to be shared in the sense they represent agreement on a matter of mutual concern. Even their ideologies and moral perspectives need not match up for the alliance to be fruitful for all stakeholders. Ideological and moral alignment is helpful and enhances the depth and resilience of the relationship, but it certainly does not serve as a cause for its formation or longevity. From this standpoint, only one true commonality exists among all types of alliances, formal or otherwise: the need or desire for collectivism vice individualism in advancing interests. Some consider such a conclusion as cynical; in fact, it reflects a realist approach to determining what sustains alliances. It reflects the realist notions first enunciated by Niccolò Machiavelli in the early sixteenth century and more recently championed by IR theorists and diplomats like Morgenthau, John Mearsheimer, and Henry Kissinger. Indeed, the underlying motivation for alliances—from their inception to their sustainment—stems from the fundamental realist concept of *raison d'état*, French for 'national interest'.

What place, then, does ideology have in shaping and sustaining alliances? Walt suggests

---

[131]Thucydides, *The Landmark Thucydides*, 68.

[132]Walt, *The Origins of Alliance*, 33.

43

the value of ideological solidarity among alliances revolves around the notions of commonality and like-mindedness. According to him, ideological solidarity characterizes alliances that "result from states sharing political, cultural, or other traits."[133] The greater the ideological commonalities between nations, the more likely they are to ally with each other and the more resilient those alliances will be over time. Walt suggests a number of hypotheses to support this logic, including

> (1) States with similar domestic ideologies are more likely to ally; (2) centralized and hierarchical movements will have greater difficulty in forming alliances, and those they do form will be more fragile; (3) ideological alignments are more prevalent in a bipolar international system; (4) states that lack domestic legitimacy will be more likely to align ideologically in order to facilitate external support as well as internal support for the regime; and (5) the impact of ideology on alliances is frequently exaggerated by statesmen and they will overestimate the degree of ideological agreement among their allies and adversaries.[134]

These hypotheses are interesting in the context of the legitimating capacity of alliances, but his final point probably bears the greatest resemblance to the recent American experience with alliances and strategic agreements. Moreover, common ideology is a convenient aspect of alliances but by no means an essential precondition to their formation.

Suggesting that national interests, not ideological agendas, drive alliances has tremendous implications on the notion of deriving legitimacy from moral authority. Moral authority draws upon a more constructivist notion. This dichotomy between constructivism (also known as idealism) and realism manifests itself in the form of continued tension between words and deeds in foreign policy, the former typically championing idealistic notions while the latter most often exhibit realist ideas. This speaks to the fundamental challenge America faces in projecting a benevolent image while advancing its national interests: the balance between words that seem

---

[133]Walt, *The Origins of Alliance*, 33.

[134]Miglietta, *American Alliance Policy in the Middle East, 1945-1992*, 4.

naïve and actions that seem arrogant. It further reveals the crux of the challenge to U.S. military legitimacy.

The Burden Sharing Effect of Alliances

An ever-growing concern for the U.S. military is how to sustain its current pace of expeditionary operations amidst increasing fiscal and resource austerity while maintaining its legitimacy along the way. This is a difficult and challenging task to be sure. In *War and Change in World Politics*, author Robert Gilpin says that even though the United States continues to be the "dominant and most prestigious state in the [international] system, it no longer has the power to 'govern' the system" as it has in the past.[135] Indeed, the rising costs of governing the international system have gradually outpaced the economic and military capacity of the United States to do so on its own. The irony of his assertion is that he made it in 1981, well before the end of the Cold War and the bipolar stability that characterized the international system gave way to a far more complex and interdependent system. The modern operational environment presents a far more diverse array of potential threats and security challenges. In turn, there are far more opportunities to spend political capital and expend military resources in order to address these threats and challenges. Alliances provide an alternative to shouldering this burden alone. They allow the United States to accomplish its national security and foreign policy goals more effectively and efficiently.[136]

The United States has long used foreign aid to alleviate the costly venture of power projection to advance its interests. This policy has not always been effective in engendering loyalty in the alliances that benefit from such aid, nor has it precluded direct military engagement

---

[135]Robert Gilpin, *War and Change in World Politics* (Cambridge: Cambridge University Press, 1981), 232.

[136]Leeds and Savun, "Terminating Alliances," 1119.

by the U.S. military. Nevertheless, Walt suggests foreign aid is a valuable tool to use for strengthening alliances. Specifically, he suggests "the provision of economic or military assistance will create effective allies, either by demonstrating one's own favorable intentions, by invoking a sense of gratitude, or because the recipient will become dependent on the donor…the more aid, the tighter the resulting alliance."[137] However, Walt is quick to point out that a significant foreign aid-based relationship is not the cause of alliance formation; rather, it is the consequence of alignment.[138] In other words, foreign aid can make an existing alliance more effective, but not necessarily create one in the absence of common interests.[139] More importantly, though, the use of foreign aid—while not sufficient to secure reliable commitment—enables weaker powers to better defend themselves against threats without the direct and immediate involvement of its allies. By using foreign aid as a source of empowerment, the United States accounts for its own security and national interests via U.S. aid-equipped proxies.[140]

For the U.S. military in particular, this burden sharing benefit requires commitment, calculation, and compromise. Commitment to the alliance framework begins with political and diplomatic legwork, but ends with multilateral military operations synchronized with multinational interests and centered on security cooperation to counter common threats. Calculation involves careful scrutiny of the security environment, paying particular attention to the cascading effects of misperception when aligning or allying with partners whose international standing or reputation undercuts the U.S. military's moral legitimacy. Compromise entails

---

[137]Stephen M. Walt, "Alliance Formation and the Balance of World Power," *International Security* 9, no. 4 (Spring 1985): 27.

[138]Ibid., 28.

[139]Ibid., 30.

[140]Ibid.

acceptance of disparate interests and ideologies, leveraging whatever commonality exists to address mutual security concerns. The U.S. military must exploit the mechanism of alliances to burden share. It must devise operational approaches that dovetail its operational objectives with both domestic and international foreign policy initiatives, all for the sake of building consensus and capacity among partners and potential allies.

Modern Trends in Alliance Strategy

A risky trend in America's modern alliance strategy is to favor less formal relationships, more appropriately characterized as alignments or partnerships that are loosely secured through semi-formal pacts and unenforceable security cooperation agreements.[141] These coalitions of the willing and security cooperation alignments are a significant departure from their more reliable siblings, formal alliances like NATO for example. In many cases, they borrow from "investments made in long-standing alliances without acknowledging their debt" and thereby erode the integrity of existing alliances.[142] As previously mentioned, formal alliances like NATO still serve as effective venues within which to advance American interests, most recently demonstrated by the NATO-led enforcement of a no fly zone over Libya in 2011. Yet, the United States continues to advance its interests through ad hoc or informal strategic agreements with nations like Pakistan, Israel, and India to name a few. The U.S. inclination toward informal partnerships, while historically understandable, weakens the institutional value of formal alliances. It suggests the benefits of formal alliances are not worth the hassle of wading through the formal alliance-making process. In addition, while informal alliances still portray some semblance of perceived legitimacy by way of their collectivism, they lack the legal-based legitimating strength that

---

[141]Sherwood-Randall, *Alliances and American National Security*, 7.

[142]Ibid., 3.

47

historically stems from formal alliances. Lastly, modern 'quick fix' relationships formed solely to serve short-term interests appear to contradict America's oft stated commitment to international values and inviolable principles. When these opportunistic relationships involve members of the international community that have less than stellar moral reputations, it calls into question America's reputation of moral constancy in the eyes of the international community. This, in turn, hinders attempts to invoke moral authority as a basis for legitimating U.S. military operations abroad. Indeed, short-term agenda-driven partnerships may ultimately prove counterproductive in assisting U.S. military planners and commanders with navigating the modern operational environment.

NAVIGATING THE OPERATIONAL ENVIRONMENT

America has a longstanding reputation of advancing its interests behind the guise of its benevolent ideological agendas. Whether framed in terms of Manifest Destiny as the United States expanded its territorial reach westward, or framed as the advancement of democracy and corresponding containment of Communism during the Cold War, America's national interests have always driven its foreign policy.[143] This strikes some members of the international community as wholly opportunistic and self-serving, ridicule that typically emanates from adversaries threatened by America's power and influence. Indeed, the perceived lack of constancy in its foreign policy is arguably one of the chief complaints the international community has with America. It projects an image of arrogance—even schizophrenia—in the eyes of many U.S. allies and strategic partners. However, it is largely the result of its gradual evolution in capacity and confidence from a small enclave of rebels defying British rule in the late eighteenth century to one of the main actors on the modern international stage. It is also a

---

[143]Herring, *From Colony to Superpower*, 180.

function of America's realization that benevolence 'buys' more lasting power and influence. Along the power continuum illustrated in Appendix A, benevolence effectively mutes the "overtly malign character of domination" and thereby engenders greater compliance, whether achieved as a function of perceived legitimacy or as a function of persuasion.[144] Successful foreign policy of this nature depends on the "appearance of sincerity…of seeming the dupe without being it."[145]

Accusations of opportunism and schizophrenia in its foreign policy may be unfair and disingenuous, but it is the realistic consequence of American hegemony.[146] Indeed, it is easy for the world community to ridicule the nation that Abraham Lincoln once described as "the last, best hope of earth," easy to find fault with the great "city upon a hill" upon which watchful eyes continuously survey for hints of hypocrisy.[147] There are plenty of other nations whose words and actions rarely match up, and whose interests clearly influence their foreign policy. Yet, their relative obscurity on the global scene effectively excuses their hypocrisy. In other words, our international reputation precedes the difficult task of ensuring our actions always match our words, and vice versa. Again, this only highlights the magnitude of the challenge facing U.S.

---

[144]Ikenberry, *After Victory*, 28.

[145]Henry A. Kissinger, *A World Restored: Europe After Napoleon* (New York: Grosset & Dunlap, 1964), 20.

[146]John J. Mearsheimer, *The Tragedy of Great Power Politics*, Reprint ed. (New York: W. W. Norton, 2003), 40–41. Mearsheimer argues the United States is, at best, a regional hegemon in the Western Hemisphere. The status of global hegemon is virtually impossible to achieve. Strictly defined, hegemony suggests world domination, and the United States does not dominate Europe or Northeast Asia. Consequently, Mearsheimer maintains there has never been a global hegemon, nor will there ever be one.

[147]Susan-Mary Grant, *A Concise History of the United States of America* (Cambridge: Cambridge University Press, 2012), 39, 137.

military commanders and planners trying to plan and conducts operations abroad under the constant scrutiny of the international community.

In January 2012, the President of the United States—in conjunction with the SECDEF and Chairman of the Joint Chiefs of Staff (CJCS)—unveiled the 2012 Defense Strategic Guidance. Therein, the President outlined his priorities for securing and maintaining the national defense of the United States. While his guidance directed a shift in focus toward the Asia Pacific region, it also reinforced America's continued commitment to existing strategic alliances and partnerships, particularly in the Middle East.[148] It also encouraged the forging of new partnerships where and when global challenges warranted cooperative efforts and emerged alongside collaborative opportunities.[149] Indeed, this guidance perpetuated contemporary American foreign policy that promotes burden sharing amidst limited global resources and increasing fiscal austerity. After all, such collaboration has the added benefit of establishing the legitimacy upon which the U.S. military presumably operates in the modern security environment. More importantly though, the 2012 Defense Strategic Guidance revealed America's continued adherence to *raisons d'état*—its national interests—as the driver behind its foreign policy, often veiled in ideological rhetoric. It offers a caveat to its emphasis on alliances, asserting the United States will continue to reserve the right to operate unilaterally when necessary.[150] This alone poses an interesting and unavoidable challenge for U.S. military commanders and planners trying to navigate the operational environment, particularly when legitimacy and unilateralism seem diametrically opposed to each other.

---

[148]U.S. Department of Defense, *2012 U.S. Department of Defense Strategic Guidance*, 3.

[149]Ibid., 8.

[150]Ibid., 7.

Indeed, the true intentions of American foreign policy, exposed by the alliances it secures, have cascading effects on military operations and significant implications for military legitimacy. Specifically, policy-directed collaboration with entities that appear to contradict American principles calls into question the motivations and credibility—the legitimacy—of the military instrument of U.S. national power. For an ingredient deemed crucial to military success, legitimacy must be a foremost consideration for military commanders and planners as they develop and implement their operational approach. This requires more than merely devising strict rules of engagement, the adherence to which should preserve and uphold the legitimacy of military actions. It may require compromise on the most favorable operational approach in terms of access, risk, and resources. In fact, it may drive an entirely different operational approach altogether. In short, legitimacy must be the common thread that parallels strategic direction in integrating and synchronizing the planning activities and operations throughout the operations process.[151] Moreover, military commanders and planners must orient the operational approach in a manner that nests with American foreign policy with respect to alliances but limits the collateral damage inflicted upon military legitimacy, no matter the cost. Doing so is not only feasible, but also essential.

<u>U.S. Military Exploits of the Recent Past</u>

There is no shortage of criticism for America's foreign policy practices in the Middle East. Much of the criticism actually comes from countries within that region and spans several decades of American interaction. There exists a "perennially vexing problem of the Arab and Muslim perception of the United States…one of perceived hypocrisy and double standards, the belief that the United States advocates great values, but does not behave in conformity with those

---

[151]U.S. Department of Defense, Joint Chiefs of Staff, *JP 5-0, Joint Operation Planning* (Washington, DC: Government Printing Office, August 2011), I-2.

values and, when it comes to Arab states, often acts in direct contradiction to them."[152] Of course, the 2001 U.S. military invasion of Afghanistan and subsequent 2003 invasion of Iraq by a U.S.-led military coalition of the willing only punctuated decades of regional displeasure with the United States. However, the most vexing American policy and strategic partnership by far is that between the United States and Israel.

Israel represents a strategic partnership deemed invaluable to the United States, but equally problematic in many ways. During the Cold War, Israel represented America's primary counterbalance in a region largely dominated by Soviet influence.[153] Naturally, the ideological and religious alignment between the two nations served to strengthen the relationship. However, many IR scholars suggest the U.S. alignment with Israel during the Cold War negatively impacted America's foreign policy objectives by influencing regional Arab states to align with the Soviet Union.[154] Additionally, they cite Israel as the root cause of America's broad failure with respect to its more recent foreign policy goals in the region. Specifically, the "continued failure to solve the problem of Israel's integration into the region and the delays in creating a Palestinian state both threaten major American interests."[155] They represent major obstructions to improved relations between the United States and the greater Arab and Muslim world in that region and beyond.

The continued willingness of the United States to endorse Israeli actions in the region, and, by doing so, enrage the same Arab neighbors with whom the United States simultaneously

---

[152]Stephen P. Cohen, *Beyond America's Grasp: A Century of Failed Diplomacy in the Middle East* (New York: Farrar, Straus and Giroux, 2009), 30.

[153]Miglietta, *American Alliance Policy in the Middle East, 1945-1992*, 20.

[154]Ibid. A number of Arab nations like Egypt and Syria sought Soviet-produced weapons to augment their military arsenals.

[155]Cohen, *Beyond America's Grasp*, 85.

seeks relations, is a stark reminder of how interests truly drive America's foreign policy. As

articulated in a recent Congressional Research Report outlining the U.S. commitment to Israel,

> For decades, the United States and Israel have maintained strong bilateral relations based on a number of factors, including robust domestic U.S. support for Israel and its security; shared strategic goals in the Middle East; a mutual commitment to democratic values; and historical ties dating from U.S. support for the creation of Israel in 1948. U.S. foreign aid has been a major component in cementing and reinforcing these ties. Although successive Administrations have disapproved of some Israeli policies…U.S. officials and many lawmakers have long considered Israel to be a reliable partner in the region, and U.S. aid packages for Israel have reflected this belief.[156]

The continuous U.S. foreign assistance of Israel to maintain Israel's qualitative military edge

(QME) in the region emboldens Israeli actions and further exacerbates Arab views of U.S.

influence in the region (Appendix D).[157] As recently as November 2012, the United States

reaffirmed its regional loyalties by siding with Israel during Israel's short but intense standoff

with Hamas and the Palestinians. As expected, the U.S. position infuriated the Arab states

sympathetic to the Palestinians' plight. A subsequent U.S. intelligence assessment concluded that

the United States undermined its ongoing outreach to Muslim countries by siding with Israel.[158]

The U.S. complicity with what the Arab world considered a disproportionate military response by

the Israelis weakened U.S. credibility in the region. Indeed, such policy decisions greatly

challenge ongoing U.S. military efforts to secure stable and productive relations with other Arab

---

[156]U.S. Library of Congress, CRS, *U.S. Foreign Aid to Israel,* by Jeremy M. Sharp, CRS Report RL33222 (Washington, DC: Office of Congressional Information and Publishing, March 12, 2012), 1.

[157]Ibid., 4. According to this CRS Report, Israel stands as the largest cumulative recipient of U.S. foreign assistance since World War II, aid totaling over $115B as detailed in Appendix D of this monograph.

[158]John McCreary, ed., "NightWatch 20121119," Kforce Government Solutions, http://www.kforcegov.com/Services/IS/NightWatch/NightWatch_12000216.aspx (accessed November 20, 2012).

players in the region, let alone facilitate any improvement to perceptions of American legitimacy among Muslims in that part of the world.

Perhaps one of the more contentious contradictions of recent American foreign policy in the region has to do with nuclear weapons. For several years now, the United States and Israel have vigorously opposed Iran's pursuit of nuclear technology, asserting Iran's true intent is to gain a nuclear weapons capability. They cite a nuclear-weaponized Iran as the first step toward a regional nuclear arms race. They further argue a nuclear Iran signifies an unacceptable risk that WMD will find its way into the hands of state-sponsored terrorist organizations operating in the Middle East and elsewhere in the world. The United States has made it clear to all regional Arab states that "American support for Arab-Israeli peace efforts rests on the preservation of Israel's security and U.S. commitments to guard Israel against an Iranian nuclear threat remain robust."[159]

Israel's policy of strategic opacity (also called deliberate ambiguity) over its possession of nuclear weapons exacerbate perceptions of legitimacy, not just for Israel but also for its closest strategic partner—the United States. The policy of nuclear opacity, or in Hebrew, *amimut*, neither acknowledges nor denies the possession of nuclear weapons, thereby exploiting the deterrent advantage of nuclear weapons without pressuring regional neighbors to acquire nuclear weapons themselves.[160] By using a policy predicated on suggestion rather than acknowledgement, Israel harnesses the power of doubt and leverages the unknown to enhance its strategic depth.[161] As

---

[159]Aram Nerguizian, U.S.-Iranian Competition in the Levant - I: Competing Strategic Interests and the Military and Asymmetric Dimensions of Regional Instability (Washington, DC: Center for Strategic & International Studies, January 10, 2013), 7, http://csis.org/files/publication/121212_Iran_VIII_Levant_report_Part_1.pdf (accessed February 4, 2013).

[160]Thomas L. Friedman, "Ambiguity Seen as Central to Israeli Nuclear Strategy," *Times-News (Hendersonville, NC)*, November 10, 1986.

[161]Shlomo Aronson and Oded Brosh, *The Politics and Strategy of Nuclear Weapons in the Middle East: Opacity, Theory, and Reality 1960-1991: An Israeli Perspective* (Albany, NY:

Avner Cohen, author of *The Worst-Kept Secret: Israel's Bargain with the Bomb*, explains, "Israel has committed to both resolve and caution…a sleight of hand that allows Israel to live in the best of all possible worlds by having the bomb but without having to deal with many of the negative consequences that such possession entails."[162] Despite mounting international pressure to get in step with global nuclear nonproliferation efforts, it is a policy the Israelis are not eager to abandon anytime soon simply because it has worked so well for so long. Proponents of such nonproliferation efforts contend Israel's position is unsustainable,

> And although global concerns about nuclear weapons in the Middle East are focused on Iran's imminent acquisition of nuclear weapons rather than Israel's 'bomb in the basement,' there is also widespread support for dealing with this problem in an evenhanded manner, namely, by establishing a NWFZ in the region…A loosening of Israel's decades-old policy of opacity would allow Israel to become a fuller partner in the international nonproliferation regime, improve its image as a responsible nuclear power, and enhance its democratic transparency at home by informing the Israeli public about the fateful decisions that are being made on its behalf regarding the bomb…In order to deal effectively with the new regional nuclear environment and emerging global nuclear norms, Israel must reassess the wisdom of its unwavering commitment to opacity and also recognize that international support for its retaining its military edge, including its nuclear capability, rests on its retaining its moral edge.[163]

The ancillary effect of Israel's policy of nuclear opacity is that it unnecessarily taints perceptions of American legitimacy in the region, particular with respect to ongoing U.S. coercive efforts to convince Iran to abandon its pursuit of nuclear weapons. In turn, this erodes U.S. military legitimacy by conjuring perceptions of hypocrisy and questionable moral authority, making it all the more difficult to design operations that promulgate a perception of legitimacy.

SUNY Press, 1992), 5.

[162] Avner Cohen, *Worst-Kept Secret: Israel's Bargain with the Bomb* (New York: Columbia University Press, 2010), xxxiii.

[163] Avner Cohen and Marvin Miller, "Bringing Israel's Bomb Out of the Basement," *Foreign Affairs* 89, no. 5 (September/October 2010): 44.

Though used to preserve freedom of action by remaining uncommitted and deliberately vague about capabilities and intentions, these policies more often set the conditions for mistrust among international actors. They create the perception there is something to hide. As a result, international actors analyze other behavioral cues and actions to decipher intent and reduce ambiguity. This has the high probability of strategic miscalculation and, in turn, may bring about unintended consequences. If a nation is trying to preserve or propagate the image of adhering to international standards of moral conduct, then a lack of transparency is hardly helpful to this cause. In short, policies of strategic opacity are not conducive to securing legitimacy. Worse, America's close alignment with key allies and strategic partners that espouse such policies makes it difficult for the U.S. military to distance itself from the delegitimizing effects of those policies. In other words, Israel's contentious policy of strategic opacity negatively affects U.S. military legitimacy in the Middle East, precisely because the two nations maintain such a close strategic relationship. The interconnectivity of strategic partnerships and international alliances allows the policies of one nation to adversely impact the legitimacy of another. This is precisely the focus of this monograph and the key challenge for military commanders and planners to overcome.

U.S. Military Endeavors of Today and Tomorrow

The security cooperation agreement between the United States and Pakistan is yet another contentious relationship with long-term ramifications for U.S. legitimacy. Unlike America's relationship with Israel and the challenges it poses for U.S. military legitimacy in the Middle East, its relationship with Pakistan serves immediate interests related to ongoing military operations in Afghanistan. It also stands as one of the more blatant examples of interests trumping ideologies as a foundation for partnership. Appendix F outlines the stated principles and purposes behind America's relationship with Pakistan. For the United States, the relationship offers regional access by land, sea, and air to conduct ongoing military operations in Afghanistan. For

Pakistan, it offers a continued source of fiscal and military aid (Appendix E) as well as the ancillary benefit of U.S. military presence to counterbalance the persistent threat posed by India on its eastern borders.[164]

The U.S.-Pakistan relationship stretches back nearly 65 years, during which time the United States has contributed significant amounts of foreign aid (Appendix E), albeit in wildly fluctuating amounts.[165] Trouble repeatedly arises in its relationship when the collective pursuit of shared interests between the two nations tramples upon Pakistan's sovereignty or compels Pakistan to deviate from its domestic ideological adherence. In other words, Pakistan's cooperation with the United States undermines its domestic legitimacy and, therefore, limits the extent to which Pakistan can appear committed to its partnership with the United States. Pakistan remains vulnerable to a domestic backlash that results from the perceived mismatch between words and actions. Further challenging the Pakistani government's attempts to establish its domestic legitimacy is the regional—even international—perception that the Pakistani military acts as a proxy for America's counterterrorism initiatives. Collaborating with America is certainly no help to Pakistan's pursuit of domestic legitimacy. Additionally, Pakistan's public response to America's periodic operations inside Pakistan's borders does not engender positive relations between the two—diplomatically or militarily—and highlights the unstable nature of their partnership. Continued American disregard for Pakistani sovereignty only weakens an already precarious partnership, punctuated by U.S. drone strikes in the tribal—but ostensibly sovereign— territories of northwest Pakistan as well as the highly publicized Osama Bin Laden raid in 2011.

---

[164]Interestingly, India receives nearly eighty-four times more in military aid and equipment via foreign military sales (FMS) agreements made in 2011 than what Pakistan receives according to the same agreements referenced in Appendix B.

[165]U.S. Library of Congress, CRS, *Pakistan: U.S. Foreign Assistance,* by Susan B. Epstein and K. Alan Kronstadt, CRS Report R41856 (Washington, DC: Office of Congressional Information and Publishing, October 4, 2012), 1.

That event alone "severely angered Pakistanis and embarrassed the Army, which was domestically seen as unable to secure the homeland against foreign intrusion and internationally suspected of providing refuge to America's worst enemy."[166]

As the United States wades through its own domestic fiscal challenges, senior leaders in the U.S. government think it is time to re-evaluate our commitment to Pakistan given its fickle behavior and questionable reliability as a U.S. ally.[167] Some suggest "sidelining Pakistan and giving India a larger stake in Afghanistan," a proposition which understandably angers Pakistan given their long-standing conflict with India.[168] Still others maintain it is important to uphold a relationship with Pakistan because it represents a critical enabler to U.S. counterterrorism effort. Meanwhile, Pakistan undergoes its own domestic struggle centered on establishing a stable and legitimate government and improving its relationship with its military. Their internal debate over the future of U.S.-Pakistani relations vacillates between complete disengagement and a renegotiation of the rules of engagement.[169] To a large degree, the lack of a cohesive and reliable alliance between the two nations stems from the absence of a common threat or common driver. The United States sees the alliance as a mechanism to support its primary counterterrorism interest in the region, namely its war against the Taliban and al-Qaeda.[170] The Pakistanis view the alliance as a means to offset the threat posed by India as well as a means to resource its domestic agenda. Instead of a relationship grounded by common interests and bolstered by common

---

[166]Shehzad H. Qazi, "US-Pakistan Relations: Common and Clashing Interests," *World Affairs* 175, no. 1 (May/June 2012): 71.

[167]U.S. Library of Congress, CRS, *Pakistan: U.S. Foreign Assistance*, 1.

[168]Qazi, "US-Pakistan Relations," 72.

[169]Ibid.

[170]Ibid.

ideologies, the United States and Pakistan have "a one-dimensional transactional relationship centered along [largely disparate] security concerns."[171]

The U.S.-Pakistan relationship is not disposable, but it is also not sustainable on its current trajectory. In the near-term, it compromises the operational gains made by U.S and Coalition military forces in Afghanistan over the past ten years. It also introduces greater risk to whatever U.S. military presence remains in Afghanistan beyond 2014.[172] In the long-term, it risks undermining U.S. military legitimacy as it transitions its focus toward the Asia Pacific region and, in doing so, attempts to strengthen key relationships with nations like India. It also risks allowing the seeds of unrest and instability within Pakistan to flourish. As a nuclear-armed state, one of only four non-signatories to the Treaty on the Non-Proliferation of Nuclear Weapons (NPT), led by "corrupt and unaccountable leaders and institutions, with a weak economy, growing population, and a youth bulge," the conditions are there to generate a significant threat to future U.S. interests.[173] Despite extraordinary tension between the two nations, disengagement is not a viable option and does nothing to enhance U.S. military legitimacy now and in the future. If the United States abandons its stated commitment to Pakistan, then it risks projecting an image of opportunism and undermining its credibility as a reliable strategic partner. In turn, this erodes the long-term legitimacy that the U.S. military might wish to leverage as it plans and conducts military operations elsewhere in the world.

---

[171]Qazi, "US-Pakistan Relations," 72. The two countries share a common enemy in al-Qaeda, but other concerns and interests overshadow that commonality.

[172]Ibid., 78.

[173]Ibid. The other non-signatories to the NPT include Israel, India, and North Korea.

The Way Ahead for the U.S. Military

As the United States turns its strategic attention toward the Asia Pacific region, it once again finds itself in familiar territory: securing its interests abroad and shoring up regional and international support to do so. Military commanders and planners navigating this complex operational environment face another less obvious but equally significant challenge: preserving legitimacy of U.S. military action abroad while walking the tightrope of *Realpolitik*. They do so under the President's strategic guidance to incorporate U.S. allies and strategic partners in the process. Assuming legitimacy is crucial to the future success of military operations in the Asia Pacific region, this challenge has tremendous implications for the application of operational art. If foreign policy provides the canvas upon which the military must paint its operations, then the U.S. military must determine the precise picture it wishes to portray and the colors with which to paint in order to uphold legitimacy and leverage its benefits to facilitate military operations abroad. This is, indeed, a unique but unavoidable challenge for military planners and senior military leaders, whether it entails generating contingency options for the commander or conducting key leader engagements with strategic partners. Throughout the operations process, planners and commanders alike must carefully nest military operations with foreign policy in order to preserve the legitimacy of American military action. When the two cannot be reconciled, U.S. military forces must be willing and able to operate in the absence of perceived or actual legitimacy and, more importantly, prepared to accept the consequences of doing so. This type of operating environment is certainly not ideal, but it is the unfortunate consequence of the *Realpolitik* nature of American foreign policy: securing controversial partnerships that serve America's interests, regardless of whether they specifically help or hinder the U.S. military's mission.

The prospects for U.S. military legitimacy in the Pacific theater of operations are certainly not doomed to echo America's experience in the Middle East, nor are they sabotaged by the ongoing tension between the United States and Pakistan. Notwithstanding significant cultural differences between its past and future operating environments, the U.S. military stands at the crossroads of a timely opportunity to reorient its operational approach in order to address its regional interests in a manner that balances the costs and benefits of alliances with the value of legitimacy. Engaging in alliances—a priority perpetuated by the President's 2012 Defense Strategic Guidance—and propagating positive perceptions of U.S. military legitimacy is no easy balance to strike. The U.S. military has no choice but to account for legitimacy, or lack thereof, as it designs and implements its operational approach. It also has no choice but to plan and conduct its operations within the framework of alliances that U.S. foreign policy builds for it. In short, walking the operational tightrope between the two—alliances and legitimacy—is a necessary skill set for U.S. military commanders and planners navigating today's complex operating environment.

The looming operational concern for the U.S. military in the Asia Pacific region revolves around the Anti-Access/Area Denial (A2AD) threat posed by China, punctuated by ongoing strife between China and its regional counterparts over the geo-strategically significant South China Sea.[174] To counter this threat, the United States expects to leverage a multilateral approach to avert conflict and maintain free flow of maritime commerce through the global commons and the Indo-Pacific region in particular.[175] For the United States, this region represents the "economic and political engine of the 21st century" and the expected prosperity it creates will hinge on the

---

[174]Nathan Freier, *Challenges to American Access: The Joint Operational Access Concept and Future Military Risk* (Washington, DC: Center for Strategic & International Studies, January 5, 2012), under "Introduction," http://csis.org/publication/challenges-american-access-joint-operational-access-concept-and-future-military-risk (accessed February 4, 2013).

[175]Patrick M. Cronin, *Contested Waters: Managing Disputes in the East and South China Seas* (Washington, DC: Center for a New American Security, December 12, 2012), under "Introduction," http://www.cnas.org/flashpoints/bulletin/bulletin-6-contested-waters-managing-disputes-east-and-south-china-seas (accessed February 4, 2013).

ability to maintain open commerce, "the vast majority of which flows over the world's oceans."[176] More specifically, maintaining freedom of navigation throughout the East and South China Seas as well as the main regional maritime chokepoint, the Strait of Malacca, is fundamental to U.S. interests and those of the actors with which the U.S. seeks to partner. India stands as a critical albeit reluctant member of that multilateral approach, as not only a "regional economic anchor and provider of security in the broader Indian Ocean region," but also as a rising power capable of counterbalancing the increased Chinese power and influence in the region.[177] It stands to reason, therefore, that U.S. military commanders and planners will necessarily incorporate India into its operational approach. However, it also stands to reason that many of those same military commanders and planners will need to continue investing in ongoing cooperative efforts with Pakistan. The question then becomes whether or not the U.S. military can maintain legitimacy operating in either region while investing in competing alliance partnerships.

CONCLUSION

Make no mistake: power is about legitimacy, and legitimacy is about perception. True power, therefore, is about more than military might, defying the notion that "might [alone] makes right."[178] True power is also about perceived power and, in turn, influence. No better mechanism tests the mettle of influence than the art of negotiating alliances to leverage collectivism in pursuit

---

[176]Cronin, *Contested Waters,* under "Introduction".

[177]S. Amer Latif, *India and the New U.S. Defense Strategy* (Washington, DC: Center for Strategic & International Studies, February 23, 2012), 2, http://csis.org/publication/india-and-new-us-defense-strategy (accessed February 4, 2013). Latif notes India's inhibitions about aligning with the United States in a strategic partnership that either constricts India's strategic autonomy or entangles India in a U.S.-led "counter China" strategy.

[178]Barnes, *Military Legitimacy*, 78.

of national interests...*raisons d'état*. This was the harsh reality illustrated in the now famous Melian Dialogue recounted by Thucydides, a verse of which opened this monograph.

The strategic partnerships the United States pursues ultimately betray its true motivations, thereby challenging the rationale and authority often invoked to justify, establish, and maintain legitimacy. Its willingness to secure such relationships outside the legitimizing construct of formal alliances further challenges its claims to legitimacy. If American foreign policy remains committed to securing interest-serving partnerships that propagate this perception, then it portends continued erosion of U.S. military legitimacy. This, of course, assumes there is more to military legitimacy than the notion of might makes right. If, in fact, legitimacy is truly a fundamental component of military operations abroad, let alone a principle of joint operations— truly a 'need-to-have', not merely a 'nice-to-have'—then the U.S. military must deliberately and comprehensively incorporate it into the design of its operational approach. It must do more than just "maintain legal and moral authority in the conduct of operations" in war; moreover, it must develop the capacity to secure legitimacy as a precursor to war and potentially amidst the conduct of war.[179] It is well within the capacity of the U.S. military to not only assert power and influence but also garner power and influence by invalidating misperceptions of its illegitimacy, despite what alliances say otherwise of America's interests and intentions. Indeed, the military's actions must often speak louder than America's foreign policy words, and they must shape a narrative that upholds legitimacy and preserves the integrity of alliances. In walking the operational tightrope between the two, the inability to strike a balance may risk operational failure overall.

---

[179]U.S. Department of Defense, Joint Chiefs of Staff, *JP 3-0, Joint Operations*, A-4.

Social Control & International Order

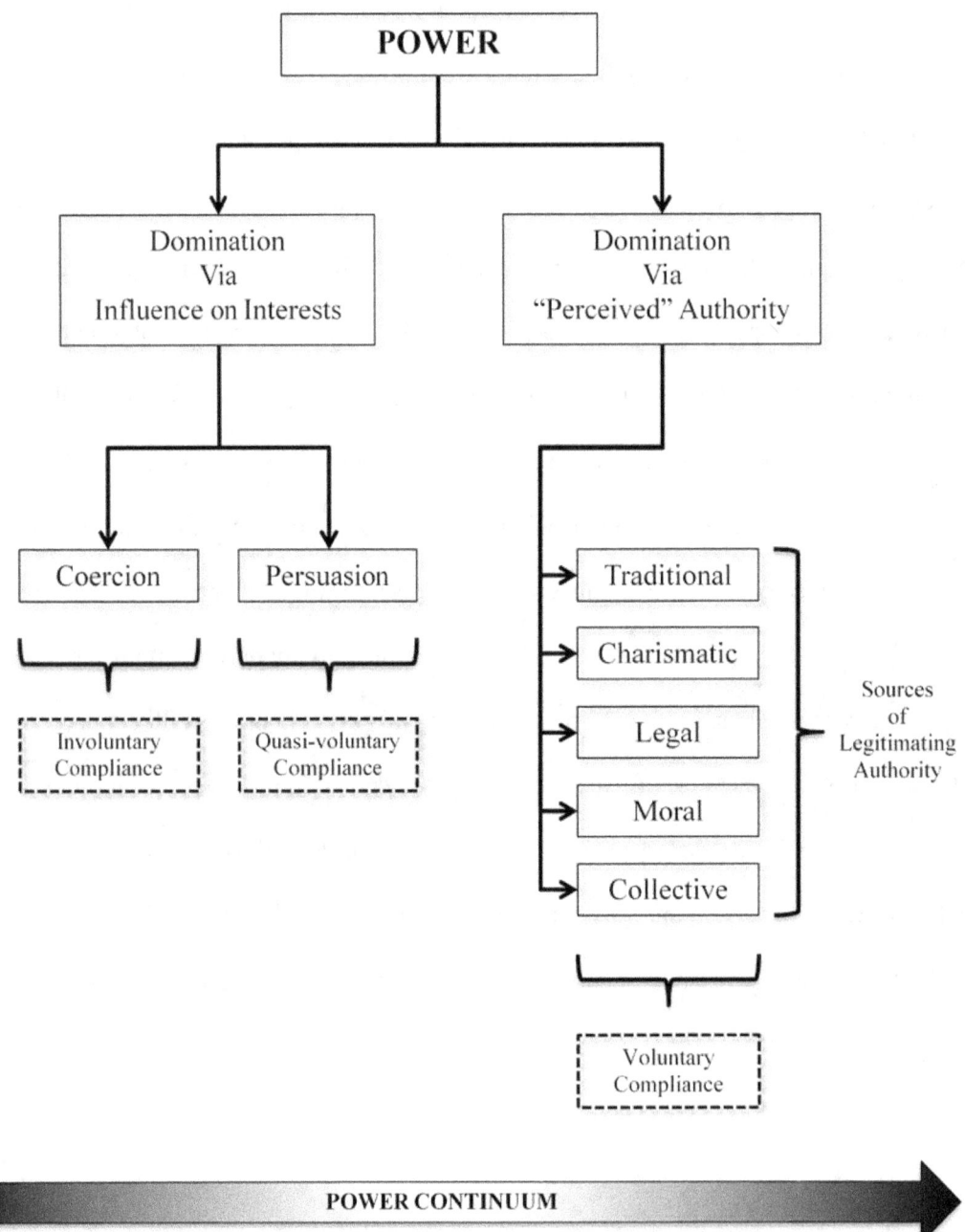

2011 U.S. Foreign Military Sales Agreements
(By Region, In Alphabetical Order)

Near East & South Asia	
Country	**Amount** **($ In thousands)**
Afghanistan	548
Bahrain	107,412
Bangladesh	1,300
Egypt	417,822
India	4,506,503
Iraq	1,940,000
Israel	1,429,361
Jordan	224,439
Kuwait	409,427
Lebanon	63,927
Morocco	11,381
Nepal	808
Oman	168,748
Pakistan	53,667
Qatar	3,014
Saudi Arabia	3,335,559
Saudi Arabia MOI	50,109
Tunisia	15,774
United Arab Emirates	1,536,024
Yemen	1,379

East Asia & Pacific Region	
Country	**Amount** **($ In thousands)**
Australia	4,028,250
Cambodia	1,279
Indonesia	38,569
Japan	601,984
South Korea (ROK)	453,015
Malaysia	49,350
Mongolia	200
New Zealand	17,053
Philippines	55,736
Singapore	377,545
Taiwan	1,939,501
Thailand	253,462
Vietnam	726

Source Department of Defense Security Cooperation Agency (DSCA), Historical Facts Book: Foreign Military Sales, Foreign Military Construction Sales and Other Security Cooperation Historical Facts, As of September 30, 2011

APPENDIX D: U.S. AID TO ISRAEL

U.S. Bilateral Aid to Israel from 1949–Present
(In millions of U.S. dollars)

Year	Total	Military Grant	Economic Grant	Immigration Grant	ASHA	All Other
1949–1996	68,030 9	29,014.9	23,122.4	868.9	121.4	14,903.3
1997	3,132 1	1,800.0	1,200.0	80.0	2 1	50.0
1998	3,080.0	1,800.0	1,200.0	80.0	---	---
1999	3,010.0	1,860.0	1,080.0	70.0	---	---
2000	4,131.85	3,120.0	949.1	60.0	2.75	---
2001	2,876.05	1,975.6	838.2	60.0	2.25	---
2002	2,850.65	2,040.0	720.0	60.0	2.65	28.0
2003	3,745.15	3,086.4	596.1	59.6	3.05	---
2004	2,687.25	2,147.3	477.2	49.7	3.15	9.9
2005	2,612.15	2,202.2	357.0	50.0	2.95	---
2006	2,534 5	2,257.0	237.0	40.0	---	0.5
2007	2,503.15	2,340.0	120.0	40.0	2.95	0.2
2008	2,423 9	2,380.0	0	40.0	3.90	0
2009	2,583 9	2,550.0	0	30.0	3.90	0
2010	2,803.8	2,775.0	0	25.0	3.80	0
2011	3,029.22	3,000.0	0	25.0	4.225	0
2012	3,095.0	3,075.0	0	20.0	---	0
2013 Requested	3,115.0	3,100.0	0	15.0	---	0
Total	**115,129.57**	**67,423.4**	**30,897.0**	**1,658.2**	**159.075**	**14,991.9**

Source Table B-1, Appendix B in U.S. Library of Congress, CRS, *U.S. Foreign Aid to Israel,* by Jeremy M. Sharp, CRS Report RL33222 (Washington, DC: Office of Congressional Information and Publishing, March 12, 2012), 30.

APPENDIX E: U.S. AID TO PAKISTAN

U.S. Bilateral Aid to Pakistan from 1948–2010
(In millions of current and constant U.S. dollars)

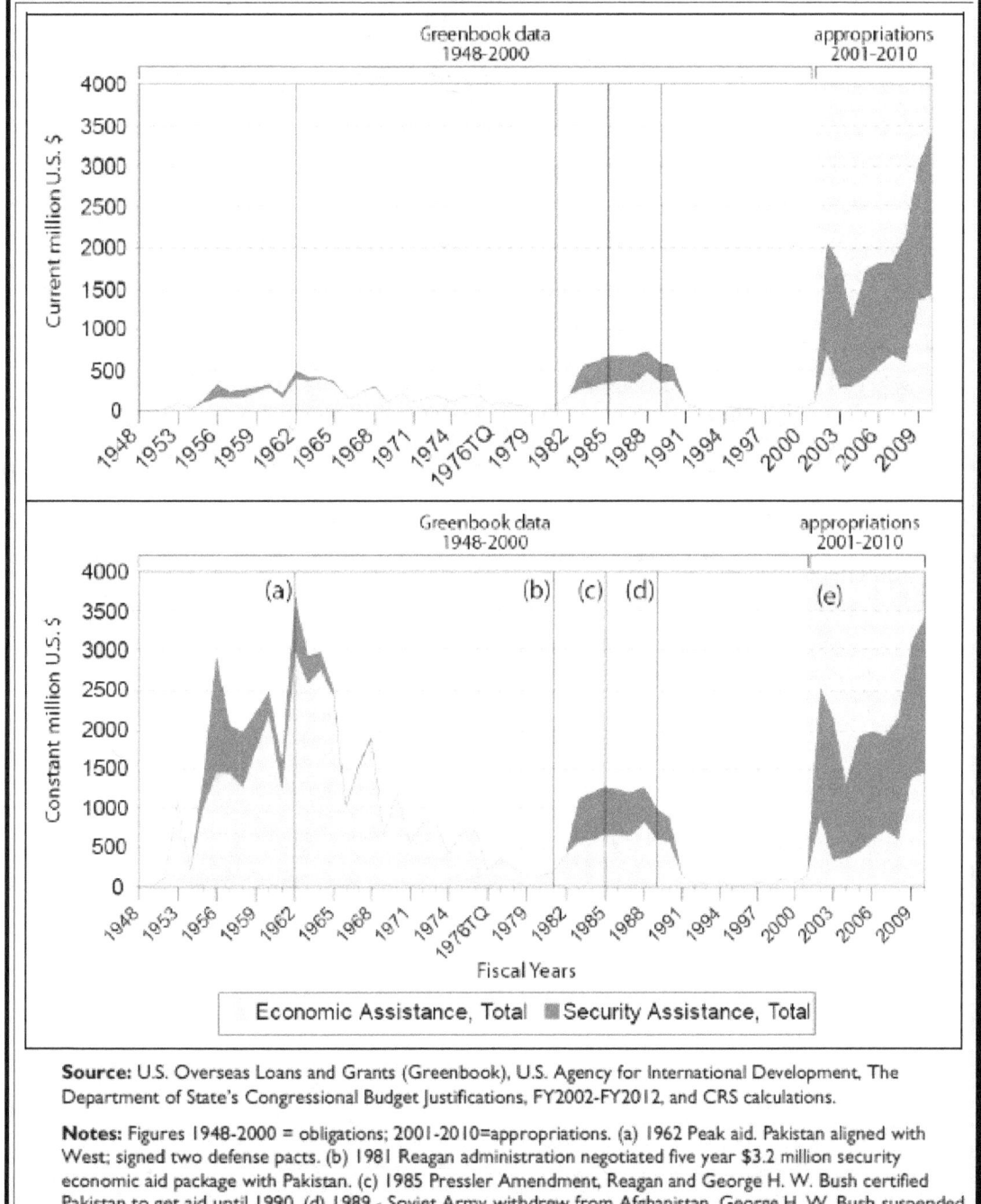

Source: U.S. Overseas Loans and Grants (Greenbook), U.S. Agency for International Development, The Department of State's Congressional Budget Justifications, FY2002-FY2012, and CRS calculations.

Notes: Figures 1948-2000 = obligations; 2001-2010=appropriations. (a) 1962 Peak aid. Pakistan aligned with West; signed two defense pacts. (b) 1981 Reagan administration negotiated five year $3.2 million security economic aid package with Pakistan. (c) 1985 Pressler Amendment, Reagan and George H. W. Bush certified Pakistan to get aid until 1990. (d) 1989 - Soviet Army withdrew from Afghanistan. George H. W. Bush suspended aid in 1990 because of Pakistan's nuclear activities. Aid lowest in 1990s. (e) Post 9/11 aid to Pakistan.

Source Figure A-1, Appendix A in U.S. Library of Congress, CRS, *Pakistan U.S. Foreign Assistance,* by Susan B. Epstein and K. Alan Kronstadt, CRS Report R41856 (Washington, DC: Office of Congressional Information and Publishing, October 4, 2012), 40.

FY2013 Budget Request for U.S. Bilateral Aid to Pakistan

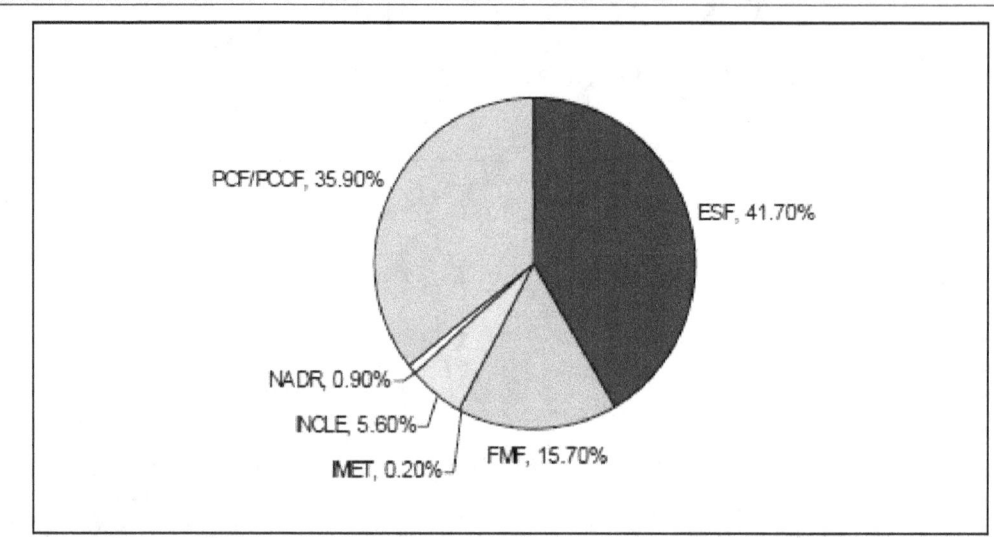

Source: The Department of State Congressional Budget Justification, FY2013 and CRS calculations.

Notes: Includes only aid from the State-Foreign Operations Appropriation Request. Defense Department funds for FY2013 are not yet available. ESF=Economic Support Fund; FMF=Foreign Military Financing; IMET=International Military Education and Training; INCLE=International Narcotics Control and Law Enforcement; NADR=Nonproliferation, Anti-terrorism, Demining, and Related Programs; and PCF/PCCF=Pakistan Counterinsurgency Fund/Pakistan Counterinsurgency Capability Fund.

Source Figure B-1, Appendix B in U.S. Library of Congress, CRS, *Pakistan U.S. Foreign Assistance,* by Susan B. Epstein and K. Alan Kronstadt, CRS Report R41856 (Washington, DC: Office of Congressional Information and Publishing, October 4, 2012), 40.

APPENDIX F: PRINCIPLES AND PURPOSES OF U.S.-PAKISTAN PARTNERSHIP

Principles and Purposes of the Enhanced Partnership with Pakistan Act of 2009

Principles:
1. Pakistan is a critical friend and ally to the United States and share goals of combating terrorism, firmly establishing democracy and rule of law, and promoting social and economic development in Pakistan;
2. U.S. aid to Pakistan is to supplement, not replace, Pakistan's own efforts;
3. The United States requires a balanced, countrywide strategy that provides aid throughout the country;
4. The United States supports Pakistan's struggle against extremism and recognizes its sacrifices in this regard;
5. The United States intends to work with the Government of Pakistan
   a. to build mutual trust by strengthening mutual security, stability, and prosperity of both countries;
   b. to support the people of Pakistan and democracy there, including strengthening its parliament, judicial system, and rule of law in all provinces;
   c. to promote sustainable long-term development and infrastructure projects, including healthcare, education, water management, and energy programs;
   d. to ensure all people of Pakistan have access to public education;
   e. to support curricula and quality of schools throughout Pakistan;
   f. to encourage public-private partnerships in Pakistan top support development;
   g. to expand people-to-people engagement between the United States and Pakistan;
   h. to encourage capacity to measure program success and increase accountability;
   i. to help Pakistan improve its counterterrorism financing and anti-money laundering;
   j. to strengthen Pakistan's counterinsurgency/counterterrorism strategy to prevent any territory of Pakistan from becoming a base for terrorist attacks;
   k. to aid in Pakistan's efforts to strengthen law enforcement and national defense forces under civilian leadership;
   l. to have full cooperation on counterproliferation of nuclear weapons;
   m. to assist Pakistan in gaining control and addressing threats in all its areas and along its border; and
   n. to explore ways to consult with the Pakistani-American community.

Purposes of Democratic, Economic, and Development Assistance:
1. To support democratic institutions in Pakistan to strengthen civilian rule and long-term stability;
2. to support Pakistan's efforts to expand rule of law, build capacity, transparency, and trust in government, and promote internationally recognized human rights;
3. to support economic freedom and economic development in Pakistan such as investments in water resource management systems, expansion of agricultural and rural development (i.e., farm-to-market roads), and investments in energy;
4. to invest in people, particularly in women and children, regarding education, public health, civil society organizations, and to support refugees; and
5. to strengthen public diplomacy to counter extremism.

Purposes of Security Assistance:
1. To support Pakistan's paramount national security need to fight and win the ongoing counterinsurgency within its borders;
2. to work with the Pakistani government to improve Pakistan's border security and control and help prevent any Pakistani territory from being used as a base or conduit for terrorist attacks in Pakistan, or elsewhere;
3. to work in close cooperation with the Pakistani government to coordinate action against extremist and terrorist targets; and
4. to help strengthen the institutions of democratic governance and promote control of military institutions by a democratically elected civilian government.

Source Appendix D in U.S. Library of Congress, CRS, *Pakistan U.S. Foreign Assistance,* by Susan B. Epstein and K. Alan Kronstadt, CRS Report R41856 (Washington, DC: Office of Congressional Information and Publishing, October 4, 2012), 43–44.

BIBLIOGRAPHY

Anderson, Benedict. *Imagined Communities: Reflections on the Origin and Spread of Nationalism*. London: Schocken Books, 1983.

Aronson, Shlomo, and Oded Brosh. *The Politics and Strategy of Nuclear Weapons in the Middle East: Opacity, Theory, and Reality 1960–1991: An Israeli Perspective*. Albany, NY: SUNY Press, 1992.

Ashforth, B.E., and B.W. Gibbs. "The Double-Edge of Organizational Legitimation." *Organization Science* 1, no. 2 (1990): 177–94.

Bajoria, Jayshree. "Libya and the Responsibility to Protect." *Council on Foreign Relations Analysis Brief* (March 24, 2011): under "first paragraph." http://www.cfr.org/libya/libya-responsibility-protect/p24480 (accessed November 23, 2012).

Barnes, Jr., Rudolph C. *Military Legitimacy: Might and Right in the New Millennium*. London: Frank Cass, 1996.

Bassiouni, M. Cherif. "International Crimes." *Law and Contemporary Problems* 59, no. 4 (Autumn 1996): 63–74.

Beres, Louis René, and Leon Edney. "Facing a Nuclear Iran, Israel Must Rethink Its Nuclear Ambiguity." *U.S. News and World Report*, February 11, 2013. http://www.usnews.com/opinion/articles/2013/02/11/facing-a-nuclear-iran-israel-must-rethink-its-nuclear-ambiguity (accessed February 23, 2013).

Berger, Peter L., and Thomas Luckmann. *The Social Construction of Reality: A Treatise in the Sociology of Knowledge*. Garden City, NY: Doubleday, 1966.

Blau, Peter M. "Critical Remarks on Weber's Theory of Authority." *American Political Science Review* 57, no. 2 (June 1963): 305–16.

Bukovansky, Mlada. *Legitimacy and Power Politics: The American and French Revolutions in International Political Culture*. Princeton: Princeton University Press, 2009.

Byman, Daniel, and Matthew Waxman. *The Dynamics of Coercion: American Foreign Policy and the Limits of Military Might*. New York: Cambridge University Press, 2002.

Clark, Ian. *Legitimacy in International Society*. New York: Oxford University Press, 2005.

Cohen, Avner. *Worst-Kept Secret: Israel's Bargain with the Bomb*. New York: Columbia University Press, 2010.

Cohen, Avner, and Marvin Miller. "Bringing Israel's Bomb Out of the Basement." *Foreign Affairs* 89, no. 5 (September/October 2010): 30–44.

Cohen, Stephen P. *Beyond America's Grasp: A Century of Failed Diplomacy in the Middle East*. New York: Farrar, Straus and Giroux, 2009.

Cronin, Patrick M. *Contested Waters: Managing Disputes in the East and South China Seas.* Washington, DC: Center for a New American Security, December 12, 2012. http://www.cnas.org/flashpoints/bulletin/bulletin-6-contested-waters-managing-disputes-east-and-south-china-seas (accessed February 4, 2013).

Daalder, Ivo H., and editor. *Beyond Preemption: Force and Legitimacy in a Changing World.* Washington, DC: Brookings Institution Press, 2007.

Dunne, Tim. "Sociological Investigations: Instrumental, Legitimist and Coercive Interpretations of International Society." *Millennium - Journal of International Studies* 30, no. 1 (January 2001): 67–91.

Ekmektsioglou, Eleni. "U.S. Military's A2/AD Challenge." The Diplomat. Entry posted January 18, 2012. http://thediplomat.com/new-leaders-forum/2012/01/18/u-s-militarys-a2ad-challenge/ (accessed March 2, 2013).

Ellis, Desmond P. "The Hobbesian Problem of Order: A Critical Appraisal of the Normative Solution." *American Sociological Review* 36, no. 4 (Aug 1971): 692–703.

Falk, Richard, Mark Juergensmeyer, and Vesselin Popovski, eds. *Legality and Legitimacy in Global Affairs.* New York: Oxford University Press, 2012.

Freedman, Lawrence. *Deterrence.* Malden, MA: Polity Press, 2004.

Freier, Nathan. *Challenges to American Access: The Joint Operational Access Concept and Future Military Risk.* Washington, DC: Center for Strategic & International Studies, January 5, 2012. http://csis.org/publication/challenges-american-access-joint-operational-access-concept-and-future-military-risk (accessed February 4, 2013).

Gaddis, John Lewis. *Surprise, Security, and the American Experience.* 1st Paperback ed. Cambridge: Harvard University Press, 2005.

Gilley, Bruce. "The Meaning and Measure of State Legitimacy: Results for 72 Countries." *European Journal of Political Research* 45, no. 3 (May 2006): 499–525.

Gilpin, Robert. *War and Change in World Politics.* Cambridge: Cambridge University Press, 1981.

Grant, Robert P. "Coalitions of the Willing: NATO and Post-Cold War Military Intervention." Final Report, NATO Public Diplomacy Division Academic Affairs Unit, 1999. In NATO Research Fellowships Programme, http://www.nato.int/acad/fellow/97-99/f97-99.htm (accessed November 24, 2012).

Grant, Susan-Mary. *A Concise History of the United States of America.* Cambridge: Cambridge University Press, 2012.

Gray, Colin S. *War, Peace and International Relations: An Introduction to Strategic History.* London: Routledge, 2007.

Hammond, James W. "Legitimacy and Military Operations." *Military Review: The Professional Journal of the U.S. Army* (July–August 2008): 61–72.

Herring, George C. *From Colony to Superpower: U.S. Foreign Relations Since 1776.* New York: Oxford University Press, 2008.

Hunter, James Davison. *Culture Wars: The Struggle to Control the Family, Art, Education, Law, and Politics in America.* Reprint ed. New York: Basic Books, 1992.

Hurd, Ian. *After Anarchy: Legitimacy and Power in the United Nations Security Council.* Princeton: Princeton University Press, 2007.

———. "Legitimacy and Authority in International Politics." *International Organization* 53, no. 2 (Spring 1999): 379–408.

Ikenberry, G. John. *After Victory: Institutions, Strategic Restraint, and the Rebuilding of Order After Major Wars.* Princeton: Princeton University Press, 2001.

———. "Institutions, Strategic Restraint, and the Persistence of American Postwar Order." *International Security* 23, no. 3 (Winter 1998/99): 43–78.

———. Review of *Legitimacy in International Society*, by Ian Clark. *Foreign Affairs* 84, no. 5 (Sep/Oct 2005): 168.

Kagan, Robert. "America's Crisis of Legitimacy." *Foreign Affairs* 83, no. 2 (Mar/Apr 2004): 65–87.

———. "Looking for Legitimacy in All the Wrong Places." *Foreign Policy* no. 137 (Jul/Aug 2003): 70–74.

Kaplan, Lawrence S. *Entangling Alliances with None: American Foreign Policy in the Age of Jefferson.* Kent, OH: Kent State University Press, 1987.

Keating, Joshua E. "America's Other Most Embarrassing Allies." *Foreign Policy* (January 31, 2011). http://www.foreignpolicy.com/articles/2011/01/31/americas_other_most_embarrassing_allies (accessed February 9, 2013).

Kissinger, Henry A. *Diplomacy.* New York: Simon & Schuster, 1994.

———. *On China.* New York: Penguin Books, 2012.

———. *A World Restored: Europe After Napoleon.* New York: Grosset & Dunlap, 1964.

Krasner, Stephen D. *Sovereignty: Organized Hypocrisy.* Princeton: Princeton University Press, 1999.

———. "Westphalia and All That." In *Ideas and Foreign Policy: Beliefs, Institutions, and Political Change*, edited by Judith Goldstein and Robert O. Keohane, 235–64. Ithaca: Cornell University Press, 1993.

Latif, S. Amer. *India and the New U.S. Defense Strategy*. Washington, DC: Center for Strategic & International Studies, February 23, 2012. http://csis.org/publication/india-and-new-us-defense-strategy (accessed February 4, 2013).

Leeds, Brett Ashley. "Alliance Reliability in Times of War: Explaining State Decisions to Violate Treaties." *International Organization* 57, no. 4 (Autumn 2003): 801–27.

———. "Do Alliances Deter Aggression? The Influence of Military Alliances On the Initiation of Militarized Interstate Disputes." *American Journal of Political Science* 47, no. 3 (July 2003): 427–39.

Leeds, Brett Ashley, and Burcu Savun. "Terminating Alliances: Why Do States Abrogate Agreements?" *Journal of Politics* 69, no. 4 (November 2007): 1118–32.

Leeds, Brett Ashley, Jeffrey M. Ritter, Sara McLaughlin Mitchell, and Andrew G. Long. "Alliance Treaty Obligations and Provisions, 1815–1944." *International Interactions* 28, no. 3 (2002): 237–60.

Levi, Margaret. *Of Rule and Revenue*. Berkeley: University of California Press, 1988.

Machiavelli, Niccolò. *The Prince*. 2nd ed. Chicago: University Of Chicago Press, 1998.

Matlary, Janne Haaland. "The Legitimacy of Military Intervention: How Important Is a Un Mandate?" *Journal of Military Ethics* 3, no. 2 (2004): 129–41.

Mead, Walter Russell. *Special Providence: American Foreign Policy and How It Changed the World*. New York: Routledge, 2002.

Mearsheimer, John J. *The Tragedy of Great Power Politics*. Reprint ed. New York: W. W. Norton, 2003.

McCreary, John, ed. "NightWatch 20121119." Kforce Government Solutions. http://www.kforcegov.com/Services/IS/NightWatch/NightWatch_12000216.aspx (accessed November 20, 2012).

McDougall, Walter. *Promised Land, Crusader State: The American Encounter with the World Since 1776*. Reprint ed. Boston: Mariner Books, 1998.

Miglietta, John P. *American Alliance Policy in the Middle East, 1945–1992: Iran, Israel, and Saudi Arabia*. Lanham, MD: Lexington Books, 2002.

Morgenthau, Hans J. *Politics Among Nations: The Struggle for Power and Peace*. 4th ed. New York: Knopf, 1967.

Morrow, James D. "Alliances and Asymmetry: An Alternative to the Capability Aggregation Model of Alliances." *American Journal of Political Science* 35, no. 4 (November 1991): 904–33.

Nawaz, Shuja. *Crossed Swords: Pakistan, Its Army, and the Wars Within*. Karachi: Oxford University Press, 2008.

Nerguizian, Aram *U.S.-Iranian Competition in the Levant - I: Competing Strategic Interests and the Military and Asymmetric Dimensions of Regional Instability*. Washington, DC: Center for Strategic & International Studies, January 10, 2013. http://csis.org/files/publication/121212_Iran_VIII_Levant_report_Part_1.pdf (accessed February 4, 2013).

North Atlantic Treaty Organization. "A Short History of NATO." http://www.nato.int/history/nato-history.html (accessed February 24, 2013).

Nye, Joseph S., Jr. *The Paradox of American Power: Why the World's Only Superpower Can't Go It Alone*. New York: Oxford University Press, 2003.

———. *Soft Power: The Means to Success in World Politics*. New York: PublicAffairs, 2005.

Orr, Robert C. *Winning the Peace: An American Strategy for Post-Conflict Reconstruction*. Washington, DC: Center for Strategic & International Studies, 2004.

Pant, Harsh V. *Understanding India's Interest in the South China Sea: Getting Into the Seaweeds*. Washington, DC: Center for Strategic & International Studies, December 18, 2012. http://csis.org/publication/understanding-indias-interest-south-china-sea-getting-seaweeds (accessed February 4, 2013).

Partridge, P. H. *Consent and Consensus*. London: Pall Mall Press, 1971.

Qazi, Shehzad H. "US-Pakistan Relations: Common and Clashing Interests." *World Affairs* 175, no. 1 (May/June 2012): 71–78.

Reiter, Dan. *Crucible of Beliefs: Learning, Alliances, and World Wars*. Ithaca: Cornell University Press, 1996.

Reus-Smit, Christian. "International Crises of Legitimacy." *International Politics* 44, no. 2–3 (2007): 157–74.

Reus-Smit, Christian, and Duncan Snidal, eds. *The Oxford Handbook of International Relations*. New York: Oxford University Press, 2008.

Rogers, Reese S. "Alliances and Coalitions of the Willing: U.S. Legitimacy in Future Conflict." Master's thesis, U.S. Army War College, Carlisle Barracks, PA, 2010.

Rothstein, Robert L. *Alliances and Small Powers*. New York: Columbia University Press, 1968.

Santana, Adele. "Three Elements of Stakeholder Legitimacy." *Journal of Business Ethics* 105, no. 2 (2012): 257–65.

Sherwood-Randall, Elizabeth. *Alliances and American National Security*. Carlisle Barracks: SSI, U.S. Army War College, 2006.

Snidal, Duncan. "The Limits of Hegemonic Stability Theory." *International Organization* 39, no. 4 (Autumn 1985): 579–614.

Snyder, Glenn H. *Alliance Politics*. Ithaca: Cornell University Press, 2007.

Suchman, Mark C. "Managing Legitimacy: Strategies and Institutional Approaches." *Academy of Management Review* 20, no. 3 (Jul 1995): 571–610.

Thucydides. *The Landmark Thucydides: A Comprehensive Guide to the Peloponnesian War*. New York: Free Press, 1998.

Tilly, Charles. *Coercion, Capital, and European States, A.D. 990–1992*. Cambridge, MA: Blackwell, 1992.

———. "War Making and State Making as Organized Crime." In *Bringing the State Back In*, edited by Peter Evans, Dietrich Rueschemeyer, and Theda Skocpol, 169–87. Cambridge: Cambridge University Press, 1985.

Tzu, Sun. *The Art of War*. Translated by Samuel B. Griffith. Oxford: Oxford University Press, 1971.

United Nations. "The Universal Declaration of Human Rights." http://www.un.org/en/documents/udhr/index.shtml (accessed January 1, 2013).

U.S. Department of Defense. Joint Chiefs of Staff. *JP 3-0, Joint Operations*. Washington, DC: Government Printing Office. August 2011.

———. Joint Chiefs of Staff. *JP 3-16, Multinational Operations*. Washington, DC: Government Printing Office. March 2007.

———. Joint Chiefs of Staff. *JP 5-0, Joint Operations Planning*. Washington, DC: Government Printing Office. August 2011.

———. *2012 U.S. Department of Defense Strategic Guidance*. Washington, DC: U.S. Department of Defense, 2012.

U.S. Library of Congress. Congressional Research Service. *Pakistan: U.S. Foreign Assistance,* by Susan B. Epstein and K. Alan Kronstadt. CRS Report R41856. Washington, DC: Office of Congressional Information and Publishing, October 4, 2012.

———. Congressional Research Service. *U.S. Foreign Aid to Israel,* by Jeremy M. Sharp. CRS Report RL33222. Washington, DC: Office of Congressional Information and Publishing, March 12, 2012.

Walt, Stephen M. "Alliance Formation and the Balance of World Power." *International Security* 9, no. 4 (Spring 1985): 3–43.

———. "In the National Interest: A New Grand Strategy for American Foreign Policy." *Boston Review* 30, no. 1 (February / March 2005). http://bostonreview.net/BR30.1/walt.php (accessed February 17, 2013).

———. *The Origins of Alliance*. Ithaca: Cornell University Press, 1990.

Waltz, Kenneth N. "Structural Realism After the Cold War." *International Security* 25, no. 1 (Summer 2000): 5–41.

Weber, Max. *The Theory of Social and Economic Organization*. Edited by Talcott Parsons. Translated by A.M. Henderson and Talcott Parsons. New York: Oxford University Press, 1947.

Wendt, Alexander. "Anarchy Is What States Make of It: The Social Construction of Power Politics." *International Organization* 46, no. 2 (Spring 1992): 391–425.

———. "Collective Identity Formation and the International State." *American Political Science Review* 88, no. 2 (June 1994): 384–96.

———. "Constructing International Politics." *International Security* 20, no. 1 (Summer 1995): 71–81.

———. *Social Theory of International Politics*. Cambridge: Cambridge University Press, 1999.

Wilcox, Jonathan P. "Legitimacy in the Conduct of Military Operations." In *Short of General War: Perspectives On the Use of Military Power in the 21st Century*, edited by Harry R. Yarger, 9–22. Carlisle, PA: U.S. Army War College, Strategic Studies Institute, April 2010.

Zakaria, Fareed. "Our Way: The Trouble with Being the World's Only Superpower." *New Yorker* 78, no. 31 (Oct 14 & 21, 2002): 72–81.

www.ingramcontent.com/pod-product-compliance
Lightning Source LLC
Chambersburg PA
CBHW081846280526
45789CB00007B/2589